A GUIDE TO GOWER

EDITORS
Don Strawbridge
Peter J. Thomas

PHOTOGRAPHY
Harold Grenfell

ORIGINAL ILLUSTRATIONS BY
A. J. Lavender

A GOWER SOCIETY PUBLICATION

'A Guide to Gower' was first prepared in 1965 by the Publications Committee of the Gower Society which then consisted of Evan Evans, Bernard Morris, T. R. Owen and J. Mansel Thomas (editor).

The Guide was revised & updated during 1998-99 by Don Strawbridge & Peter Thomas. This sixth edition builds on previous editions whilst reflecting the many changes that have taken place since the previous editions were produced. The latest work was guided by a Steering Committee of the Gower Society consisting of: Gary Gregor, Malcolm & Ruth Ridge, Don Strawbridge & Peter Thomas.

1st edition	September	1965
2nd edition	March	1966
reprinted	April	1969
reprinted	August	1971
3rd edition	April	1973
reprinted	January	1975
4th edition	April	1979
5th edition	April	1982
reprinted	January	1985
reprinted	January	1989
reprinted	July	1990
6th edition	May	1999
reprinted	August	2009

The editors gratefully acknowlege the work of their predecessors and wish to thank all the authors of the articles, which have been fully revised.

Thanks also to the following for their help with this sixth edition: Rod Cooper for his notes on the entries for North East Gower; Malcolm Ridge and Gary Gregor for updated comments on a number of the entries.

Also, Marion Davies & Graham Wattley for checking and proof-reading prior to publication.

ISBN 978 0 902767 23 2

Published by
The Gower Society
c/o Swansea Museum, Victoria Road, Swansea, SA1 1SN

Printed by
Dinefwr Press, Rawlings Road, Llandybie, Carms., SA18 3YD

CONTENTS

Front cover photographs:
Three Cliff Bay; Penrice Church; Gower pony; Sea pinks.

INTRODUCTION

Welcome . . .

The sixth edition of 'A Guide to Gower' is aimed to interest holiday makers and day visitors to the peninsula as well as residents of both Swansea and Gower.

The backbone of Gower is the main sandstone ridge which separates the north from the south; it rises to just over 600 feet at Cefn Bryn and Rhossili Down. Such areas provide excellent panoramic viewpoints over Gower and on a good day as far as Pembrokeshire and Devon.

Due to the variety of scenery, flora and wildlife, it is a surprise to a large number of people that the peninsula covers such a relatively small area; it is only 18 miles east to west and varies between 3 and 8 miles across north to south. In 1956 it was the first place in Britain to achieve the Area of Outstanding Natural Beauty (A.O.N.B.) status. The peninsula's uniqueness is further emphasised by being the location of three National Nature Reserves, many Glamorgan Wildlife Trust Reserves, a large number of Sites of Special Scientific Interest and 136 acres (55 hectares) of Heritage Coast, with the National Trust the largest land owner. The commons, which cover 20% of the peninsula, are being considered as Special Areas of Conservation under an E.E.C. Habitat Directive.

Such official recognition is welcomed but, to many visitors, the lasting memories are of Gower's south coast stretching west from Swansea. At first, there are a number of popular, easily reached bays such as Limeslade, Bracelet, Langland and Caswell. Then the coast becomes more rugged with magnificent cliff scenery, coming to a climax with the aptly named promontory, Worms Head. At the foot of the limestone cliffs are some excellent bays and coves: such as Brandy Cove and Mewslade. Larger beaches like Oxwich and Rhossili are unforgettable sweeps of unbroken sand. It must be remembered however, that after Caswell, apart from Oxwich and Port Eynon, the bays are not directly accessible by car; but even looking down onto the beach at Rhossili is memorable.

The dunes or burrows which fringe many of the bays like Three Cliff, Pobbles and Oxwich have many delights. While on the top of the grassy cliffs, there are walks to enjoy and both sea and country views. In the limestone cliffs, there are numerous bone caves; the most important of which is Paviland; many of the caves, however, are difficult to access.

The other side of Gower, the north coast, is very different in scenery and character but has a charm and beauty of its own. The Burry Estuary with its tidal sandflats and salt marshes has a great variety of physical features and animal life, all adapted to constantly changing tidal conditions. Although bathing can be dangerous, this coast has a number of sandy bays and extensive dunes, mainly around the Whiteford area. There are walks starting from Llandmadoc, Llangennith and Whiteford, all of which highlight the particular delights of this coast.

Many villages in the peninsula have interesting features: the church, usually Norman in character or the chapel (many established by the formidable Lady Barham), the village green or the characteristic houses. There are traces of human habitation from almost every period since prehistoric times. The countryside is dotted with standing stones and megaliths, some of which, like Arthur's Stone, have a variety of explanations and legends. The castles have a fascinating history, as have more recent industrial relics: the ruins of old mills, an old salthouse and numerous lime kilns. Former railway tracks such as those along Swansea Bay and up Clyne Valley give facilities for walking and cycling.

Business is still present in the peninsula, often linked to a particular attribute of Gower: for example, the cockle industry, famous around Penclawdd and now with a processing plant at Crofty; others like the Farming Co-operative, the spring-water facilities, poultry farms, pick-your-own fruit farms, garden centres, farm shops and holiday accommodation, all help the local economy, but are of such a size and type not to harm the environment.

Overall, the area is largely undeveloped and unspoilt, thanks mainly to the Local Authority working in partnership with the Gower communities and national and local voluntary organisations. So the peninsula is not for the visitor with a wish for highly sophisticated entertainment. Gower has no cinema, railway or motorway, yet the absence of such features of modern society, linked to the natural features, give the peninsula its own special atmosphere. In the summer, this is helped by a Classical Music Festival held mainly in the churches, the Folk Festival held in many Gower locations and the long standing one-day Agricultural Show held at the airport on Fairwood Common.

The stranger to Gower can begin to use this Guide by checking in the Gazetteer some of the places mentioned in this introduction; others might wish to look up a specific place, to check its location, special features etc.; there are around 250 places so covered. If greater detail is required there are fourteen special articles on various aspects of Gower, written by experts. Two other features of the Guide are the Reference Section with its facts and figures and a pull-out map, retained from previous editions, at the back of the book. If any errors are seen in this edition, the editors would welcome amendments or additional information for possible inclusion in future editions.

As with other Gower Society publications, profits from the sale of this guide will be used to help the work of the Society.

Since 1965, the Guide has sold over 30,000 copies and justifiably earned much praise for its contributors; it is hoped that you will enjoy reading this updated and enlarged edition and that it furthers your enjoyment of Gower.

The Editors

GAZETTEER

EDITORS' NOTE:

In this edition of A Guide to Gower for the selection of places for major entries in the Gazetteer and for the spelling of these place names, the Ordnance Survey 1:25,000 Explorer 10 (164) map of Gower was used. Some other places of interest, not shown on the map, are cross referenced to an associated map location.

Population figures *are based on the Electoral Roll of 1995, so the population numbers include only the electorate.*

Place Names *in bold, italic type in the text have entries in the Gazetteer.*

Figures *following an entry are Ordnance Survey Grid References.*

ABBREVIATIONS USED			
CP	car park		
FP	footpath	NT	National Trust
PO	post office	HWM	high water mark
PH	public house	LWM	low water mark
SwM	Swansea Museum	AONB	Area of Outstanding Natural Beauty
BM	British Museum	Listed G II or G III	Reference to the listing and grading of an historic building by CADW
NatMW	National Museum of Wales, Cardiff	TIC	Tourist Information Centre

ABER-LOGIN Originally a solitary farm on the *Loughor* estuary to the west of *Wernffrwd*. First recorded in the 17th century, the name is the only instance on the Ordnance Survey map of Gower of the Welsh 'aber', which carries the meaning 'estuary' and can also refer to the mouth of a river or the confluence of two streams. *Abercedi Farm* which also lies on the fringe of the estuary does not appear on the map. 'Login' derives from Welsh 'halog' meaning dirty or muddy and the name could be a reference to a muddy stream.

511938

AIRPORT, SWANSEA *see Swansea Airport*

ARTHUR'S STONE Remarkable dolmen on *Cefn Bryn*. A Neolithic chambered tomb (about 2500 BC), constructed of stone of uncertain origin. Capstone said to weigh over 25 tons. Frost, lightning, a miller in search of a millstone and King Arthur's sword have all been blamed for the split-off portion. The stone is possibly the Maen Cetti, one of the wonders of the ancient Isle of Britain. One legend tells that it was a pebble shed from King Arthur's shoe, yet another that it goes down to the sea to drink on New Year's Eve.

½m S.E. is a Holy Well, formerly part of the Gower water supply. Small cairns are scattered over the hilltop.
Reached by FP northwards from highest point of road crossing *Cefn Bryn* from *Cillibion* to *Reynoldston.*   **491906**

BACON HOLE *see Deepslade*

BANTAM BAY On E. side of *Pwlldu Head.* Location of the 'Ring Rock' and other reminders of the former export trade in limestone.   **575866**
See also Pwlldu

BARLAND CASTLE *see Barland Common*

BARLAND COMMON Open Millstone Grit moorland alongside main road directly N. of *Bishopston Valley.* Limestone quarrying near here has uncovered a few small stalactite caverns, with some prehistoric remains (in SwM). Stream disappears underground near northern edge of quarry.
Barland Castle is an early Norman period ringwork on northern edge of the common, but on private land.   **578897**

BEGGARS PIT Large sink hole, one of a series, adjacent to public footpath S. of *Hangman's Cross.* Unfortunately, there is no evidence to support the theory that it was a burial site for plague victims and/or corpses from the gibbet at *Hangman's Cross.*   **481866**

BENRICK *see Great Tor*

BERGES ISLAND N.E. tip of *Whiteford Burrows* and a popular location for bird watchers. Once one of Gower's four tidal islands, the others being *Mumbles Head, Worm's Head* and *Burry Holms.*   **448957**

BERTHLWYD A public house (which, in 1998, was not open), farms and domestic buildings between *Gowerton* and *Penclawdd.* Formerly the site of coal mines dating back to Tudor times. The largest of the mines was *Wernbwll.* During World War II there was a munitions testing range on the marshes near here.   **562964**

BERTHLWYD UCHAF A small dairy farm situated in North Gower between *Gowerton* and *Penclawdd.* The site of a small pottery in the 18th century probably using clay dug locally. Details of the pottery can be found at SwM.   **566964**

BERRY Name given to small collection of farms near *Scurlage.* Ring-work (traces only) ½m N.E.; the Berry Wood Wildlife Trust Reserve is near-by.   **472878**

BETLANDS Farm on Burry Pill 1m N.W. of *Llandewi*.   455896

BISHOPSTON (Welsh. *Llandeilo Ferwallt*). Large village (Pop. 1,662) at head of *Bishopston Valley* formerly a centre for market gardening. Now a number of private housing developments surround the old village. St. Teilo's Church. PO, 2 PHs, shops. The former Providence (English Congregational) chapel, built in 1807, is a Guide activity centre. The Joiners' Arms still brews local ales in its own brew house. The original Malt House, on Bishopston Road, has been converted into a dwelling.
Iron Age promontory fort at Backingstone (1m S.W.).
Road to *Murton* (PO, PH) (½mE.), *Kittle* (PH, shops) (½m W.)
Nearest Bays: *Caswell* (2m by road); *Brandy Cove* (1½ m), *Pwlldu* (½m) – accessible by paths only, from *Pyle Corner*.   579893

BISHOPSTON VALLEY (NT, accessible by footpaths only, not all of them easy going.) Rugged wooded valley of the Bishopston stream, winding two and a half miles from near Bishopston Church to *Pwlldu Bay*. Of considerable botanical and geological interest. The stream is partly subterranean; in wet weather flowing above ground much of the way, in dry weather it can be heard flowing underground, notably at *Guzzlehole*, halfway down the valley. Remains of Long Ash Lead Mine in valley.
Access on foot from the side road opposite *Barland Common*, *Widegate* (lane opp. Pennard Church), *Pyle Corner*, or entirely by footpath from *Pwlldu Bay*.   575892 – 574872
See Manselfield

BISHOP'S WOOD *see Caswell Valley*

'Roman Bridge', Blackpill

BLACKPILL Village suburb of Swansea on edge of sea, midway between Swansea and Mumbles. Children's playground. 'Roman' bridge (probably 18th cent.) *Clyne Castle*, a listed Grade II building, is not a true castle but was the former home of a branch of the Vivian family. Formerly known as 'Woodlands Castle' it is now a hall of residence for University of Wales,

Swansea. Grounds open to public with many rare species of rhododendrons and azaleas, many planted by Admiral Heneage-Vivian. Paddling pools on sea front. Cafe in former electrical sub station of the Mumbles Railway. *Clyne Valley* is a steep-sided, winding, wooded, valley reaching the sea at Blackpill. The area is a Country Park with a combined footpath and cycle track running along the route of the former LMS railway line to *Dunvant*. The path also links up with the path around Swansea Bay. The Valley had much industry in the past. There are remains of brick works, collieries, bell pits and chemical works scattered through the woodland. An early stretch of the Mumbles Railway can still be followed. This railway, which was the first in the world to carry passengers, was originally built to exploit the mineral wealth of the Clyne Valley and to bring coal to the docks in Swansea.

FP and cycle path on edge of sea to *Oystermouth* and Swansea, along former Mumbles Railway track. Cafes, shops, petrol, PH, PO.   **619904**

BLUE ANCHOR Community in north east Gower on hill above *Penclawdd*. The name derives from an old established public house built here on the original turnpike road leading from *Penclawdd* to *Three Crosses* and possibly dating from the construction of that road in the late 18th century.   **552951**

BLUEPOOL BAY *see Bluepool Corner*

BLUEPOOL CORNER Sandy cove when tide out; accessible on foot only; FP across dunes from Llangennith (2m) or from Burry Holms at the tip of Rhossili Bay. The Blue Pool is a circular rock pool 15ft. across, once thought to be bottomless. Numbers of gold doubloons and moidores were found near here. Very fine natural archway W. of the bay, known as *Three Chimneys*. In sand dunes nearby remains of a stone-walled Iron Age enclosure.

Two small caves near here. The cave in the cliff to the W. is known as 'Culver Hole', but see the gazetteer entry *Culver Hole*. To the E. is a small sea cavern of no special importance known as 'Cathole', but see the gazetteer entry *Cathole*.   **409930**

BOVEHILL CASTLE Above *Landimore*, ruins of castle, near a refurbished cottage. Formerly seat of Sir Hugh Johnys, Crusader and once Knight-Marshal of England.   **465933**

BRACELET BAY [from *Broad Slade*] The first of the limestone bays of Gower, after leaving Swansea Bay and rounding *Mumbles Head*. Pebbly, some sand, rock pools. A fine example of a fossil coral reef can be seen in the middle portion of the bay (just below the rim path). To W. is *Tutt Hill*, with coastguard station and major maritime rescue co-ordination centre, then *Limeslade Bay*. Walks up *Mumbles Hill* and along coast. Car parks, refreshments, toilets.   **631872**

BRANDY COVE Little inlet ½m W. of *Caswell*, probably so named by smugglers of the 18th cent. Excellent exposures of the Pleistocene raised beach, marking a time when sea level was about 30 feet higher than today. FP through wooded slade/valley (*Hareslade*) from *Pyle Corner* (1m). Lead mines once worked here. Footpath from *Caswell* (¼m E.), *Pwlldu* (1m W.). **586874**

BROAD POOL Small stretch of fresh water alongside main road crossing Cefn Bryn from N. road (B4271) at *Cillibion*. Permanent nature reserve, rich in water plants (including the rare, yellow, fringed water-lily), insect and bird-life (duck, heron, swan, grebe etc.). Water held up through subsidence of glacial boulder clay into dissolved caverns in the underlying limestone. *See also Moormills* **510910**

BROUGHTON BAY (pron. bruffton). Broad, sandy, dune-fringed bay 1m. N. of *Llangennith*, facing N.W. Access by lane from village, then footpath. Estuary tides here make bathing dangerous. In 1868 sixteen vessels outward bound from Llanelli were wrecked here on the same tide.

Marks northward emergence of the important geological fault that defines the west side of *Rhossili Down*.

FPs to *Bluepool Bay* (1m W.) and to *Whiteford Burrows* (1½m E.). **420932**

BRYN FARM A farm on Forest Common south of *Crofty*. The original name of *'Gower's Load'* may derive from a connection with the nearby coal mines from where coal was taken to all parts of the peninsula. **525933**

BRYN-SIL Farm ruin on bridleway to *Berry*, north of *Hangman's Cross*. **482871**

BULWARK, THE A large defended enclosure of Iron Age date prominently sited at the eastern end of *Llanmadoc Hill*. The surrounding banks and ditches are well preserved and are complex in plan. Their form suggests that the original defences were enlarged over a period of years. **443928**

BURRY Group of small farms on one of Gower's most characteristic lanes, in parts sunken and very narrow. Burry Lane connects *Llandewi* on the S. road (A4118) with *Burry Green* on the road to Llangennith and is the shortest road link between *Rhossili* and *Llangennith*. It runs alongside the *Burry Pill* (the nearest Gower has to a river), which reaches the sea at *Whiteford*. **458904**

BURRY ESTUARY *see Loughor, River*

BURRY GREEN Hamlet with large green facing N.W. slopes of Cefn Bryn, at junction of Burry Lane with main Swansea-Llangennith road. Once

Burry Middle Mill

North Gower centre for Calvinistic Methodists at Bethesda Chapel; the first of six chapels founded by Lady Barham (see *Fairyhill*). Inside is a memorial to Rev. William Griffiths (1788-1861), 'The Apostle of Gower'.

Cadiz Hall is a curiously named house on Burry Lane. The name certainly existed as early as 1695, and could be derived from a medieval Gower family name.

FPs to *Burry* (S.) and across *Ryers Down* (N.).   **462914**

BURRY HOLMS (Old Scandinavian holm – island). Small, limestone tidal island forming northern tip of *Rhossili Bay*. Accessible for approximately 2½ hrs. each side of low water. Rich in cliff flowers and sea birds. Ruins of medieval monastic settlement. An Iron Age earthwork, consisting of a single bank and ditch, bisects the island. The sixth cent. St. Cenydd has strong associations with this area and the medieval ruins may represent a centre of pilgrimage connected with his memory. The automatic lighthouse once here was decommissioned in 1966 and removed.   **400925**

BURRY INLET *see Loughor, River*

BURRY PILL One of the major streams of Gower, which once provided water power for seven mills. Originating from springs below *Cefn Bryn* it drains into *Loughor Estuary* near to *Berges Island*.   **450980**
See also Burry

BURRY STONES *see Knelston*

BUTTERSLADE [? from butt(e) – blunt, rounded]. *See Thurba Head*

11

BUTTER WELL *see Llanrhidian*

CADIZ HALL *see Burry Green*

CANNISLAND PARK *see Kilvrough Manor*

CARTERSFORD BRIDGE At a point on N. road (B4271) where it dips and bends into a wooded glen to cross the small Ilston Stream. Marks boundary of **Fairwood Common** with **Pengwern Common**. Once the site of a smithy.   **552914**

CASWELL BAY (? from Cresswell or cress stream). Popular, easily accessible, but still one of the most picturesque of Gower bays. Sheltered by cliffs and a fringe of pinetrees, firm sands, car-parks, refreshments, shops, toilets. The Bishop's Wood Nature Reserve and Information Centre is situated near the terminus for Swansea buses.
   The hymn-writer Frances Ridley Havergal (1836-1879) lived here briefly until her death. *See* **Newton**.
   Iron Age earthwork above W. of the bay on Redley Cliff.
   FPs. to **Langland** (1½ E.), **Pwlldu** (1m W.), via **Brandy Cove**.
   Caswell Valley is a short wooded valley with walks, entrance from CP opp. bay, to **Bishopston** (1½m N.) and **Murton** (1m N.). Ruins of *St. Peter's Chapel and Well*, believed to be the 'Porth Tulon' mentioned in a Papal Bull of 1128.   **593876**
See also Holtsfield

CATHAN Isolated group of three former farmhouses on S.W. slopes of **Hardings Down**: East, West and Middle Cathan.   **436902**

CATHOLE 1. (or Cat's Hole) An interesting inland bone-cave in **Green Cwm**, **Parkmill**, quite easily found. Follow road from near the Gower Heritage Centre in Parkmill for about a mile to car parking and then through a gate erected by the Ramblers' Association, suitable for disabled access, into the valley; pass by the megalithic tomb known as **Giant's Grave**, and 200 yards further on, climb steep slope to R. Cave about 50 feet up. Considerable remains of prehistoric occupation by man and animals in BM. Also easy access to Green Cwm from N. road (A4118) by FP. starting at **Llethrid**.
   2. *See Bluepool Corner*   **537900**

CEFN BRYN [Welsh: ridge hill] Old Red Sandstone spine of the peninsula, running WNW. from **Penmaen** to **Burry Green** (over 4 miles) The second highest point in Gower, 188m. (617ft.), its slopes dominate almost every inland view. This is the best place to scan the whole face of Gower, with its changing lights and colours and variety of landscape. In the foreground is an intricate field pattern of small well-kept farms, woods and moorland. Further to the south, the fringe of limestone cliffs and sandy bays (notably **Oxwich**

and *Three Cliff*), and, to the north, salt marshes and the estuary. In the distance, a vast expanse of the Bristol Channel with the granite Lundy Island (to S.W.); and the heights of Somerset (Exmoor), Devon (Dartmoor, Hartland Point), Pembrokeshire (Preseli Hills), Breconshire (Beacons), Carmarthenshire (the Fans).

The main route for traffic across Cefn Bryn, formerly known as the Old Coal Road (or Red Road), is from the N. road (B4271) at *Cillibion* towards *Reynoldston*.

A fine Green Way from *Penmaen* (behind the former workhouse which later became an Old People's Home, originally *Glan y môr* and then 'Three Cliffs Nursing Home'), runs the whole length of the Bryn and is a most spectacular walk. It is known as Talbot's Road. C. R. M. Talbot, a 19th century owner of Penrice Castle, made good use of it for hunting and picnicking parties. A carriageway from Penrice meets it just above *Home Farm*.

The Gower Way crosses Cefn Bryn from Penmaen to Reynoldston on its way between Penlle'r Castell and Rhossili. *The Gower Way Stone* at the eastern end of the Bryn was unveiled by HRH the Prince of Wales in 1998 to inaugurate the Gower Way. Above Reynoldston, and near where the Red Road crosses the Bryn, is a viewpoint at which stands a direction finder installed by the local Round Table to commemorate the Silver Jubilee, in 1977, of Queen Elizabeth II.   **519889**

See also Arthur's Stone, Broad Pool

CHAPEL MERE Pond in fields N. of *Horton*. Water was once carried on donkeys from here to supply the surrounding area. The origin of the name is obscure.   **474868**

Church of St. Cadog, Cheriton

CHERITON [prob. Church farm]. Tiny village (pop. 140) one mile E. of *Llanmadoc*.

The Church of St. Cadog is one of the most beautiful of the Gower churches.

The Glebe House is 15th cent., and built for the Order of Knights Hospitaller of St. John. It is the oldest inhabited building in Gower.

FPs up wooded valley to **Stembridge** (1½m S.E.). Over hill to **Llangennith** (2m S.W.) 451932

See also North Hill Tor

CILLIBION (Welsh: wet woods) Where road crossing **Cefn Bryn** branches off main N. road (1½m E. of Llanrhidian). Petrol.

The fields from Cillibion south to Cefn Bryn once belonged to Neath Abbey. ¼ mile W. of road junction is a fine Bronze Age burial mound – **Pen-y-Crug**. FPs to **Welsh Moor, Parkmill**. 516914

See also Moormills

CILIFOR TOP Prominent rounded hill of Millstone Grit ¼m E. of **Llanrhidian**. Site of large Iron Age hill fort/earthwork occupying 3ha. (8 acres); one of the most extensive in this area. Clearly seen from **Cefn Bryn,** there is access on foot from the B4295 north of the junction with B4271, also from the minor road over **Welsh Moor** west of Parc-y-rhedyn Farm. 507922

CLYNE COMMON Approx. one mile along the B4436 from its junction with the Mumbles Road at Blackpill. Open, airy moorland (of millstone grit), with fine long views of Gower, Swansea Bay and Mumbles Head. Golf course (18 holes) and many footpaths. 595900

CLYNE VALLEY *see Blackpill*

CLYNE CASTLE *see Blackpill* 615906

COCKSTREET Characteristic Gower lane, leading from **Llangennith** to **Broughton Bay**. Recalls gaming and cock-fighting days of this once lawless part of the peninsula. The original farm off Cockstreet has been converted into a number of cottages. 426920

COETY GREEN Secluded part of **Llangennith**, on the lane leading down from the church, with ruins of two or three houses. Two streams meet here, the larger, **Diles Lake**, eventually reaching the sea on Rhossili sands. The water once turned the wheels of three mills.

FPs to **Hillend** (¼m W.) and across **Rhossili Down** to **Middleton** and **Rhossili** (3m S.). 427910

COLD COMFORT *see Merrysun*

COLLEGE MILL *see Llangennith* 427914

CRABART Part of the tidal 'Shipway' between **Worms Head** and the mainland, more especially those far-out flatter rocks forming a spit eastwards towards **Tears Point** and exposed only at low tide. 401869

CRAWLEY WOODS (locally Crowley) *see Nicholaston*

CRAWLEY POINT *see Nicholaston*

CRICKTON Farm near **Llanrhidian** on northern edge of **Cefn Bryn** common. **503917**

CROFTY Original settlement dates from Tudor times. But this much-changed village on the edge of the marshes of the **Loughor Estuary** began to grow around 1880, first as a group of miners' cottages, which still stand at the centre of the original village. Now the area, with its cockle processing plant, has become the principal modern site of the north Gower cockle industry.

Zoar Presbyterian Church was built in the middle of Crofty in 1884. *Crofty Inn* was once a substantial farmhouse.

Road along edge of salt marshes to **Llanrhidian** (2m W.). **527951**

CROWDERS QUAY *see Port-Eynon*

CULVER HOLE 1. A most intriguing walled-in cave W. of Port-Eynon Point. Accessible at sea-level, but only up to half tide, by tracks around the Point and from cliff top, or from **Overton Mere** (¼m W.).

One of the mysteries of Gower is how this fantastic 60-foot wall of masönry, pierced by look-out windows, came to be built in such a remote part of the coast. From the name (O.E. culvr = pigeon) it seems to have been used as a colombarium or dove-cote, where pigeons were bred for food or, originally, a natural breeding-place for this bird; such holes may be seen above the masonry. Popular theory is that it was a smugglers' retreat, when Port-Eynon was a thriving little port. But walling suggests much earlier origin. May have been stronghold-cum-colombarium for Port-Eynon Castle, of which there is now no trace, but mentioned in law-suit records in 13th cent. (cf. similar walling at Carreg Cennen Castle, near Llandeilo). In early 16th cent., reputed that the notorious John Lucas of Salthouse repaired and rebuilt 'Kulverd Hall' and used it as a stronghold and armoury, making access to it under the Point by underground passage. 'Whereof no man knew ye mouth thereof'. **465845**

2. Bone cave of same name in N.W. Gower, 100ft. W. of Bluepool Bay. The remains of over 30 individuals were discovered here: suggests that the cave was used as a burial place during the Bronze Age. Most of remains in NatMW. **405930**

See Bluepool Corner

CWM IVY Point of access to *Whiteford Sands and Whiteford Burrows* (NT) ¼m N. of *Llanmadoc*. A small group of houses down short lane alongside Llanmadoc Church. Parking in field (*honesty box at gate*).

In Cwm Ivy Tor, left of path, is small cavern facing east. Of no recorded archaeological interest. **438937**
See Groose (The)

DEBORAH'S HOLE Small bone cave app. ½m W. of *Paviland Caves*, high in cliffs above inlet formed by *Horse Cliff* and *the Knave*.

Remains in SwM. **434863**

DEEPSLADE (NT) Pebble bay on western side of Pwlldu Head (1m E. of *Southgate* bus terminus).

Takes its better known name of 'Hunts Bay' from farm and land on cliff above, which the Norman Lord of Gower, William de Breos, presented to his huntsman, William de Hunde.

Hunts Farm lies at the head of the bay near the start of the lane to Pwll-du, along which no unauthorised vehicles are allowed.

On a rocky step, difficult of access, is a memorial to the poet Vernon Watkins, who lived nearby.

Bacon Hole is a bone-cave in cliff face W. of Deepslade. Evidence of occupation by man in Iron Age, Roman and later periods. Prehistoric animal remains, brooches, etc. in SwM. Name derived from red oxide streaks on cave wall. Path from cliff top. **563868**
See also High Pennard, Heatherslade

DELVID *Llangennith* farm overlooking *Broughton Bay* and Burrows.
424928

DEVIL'S BRIDGE *see Worms Head*

DEVIL'S KITCHEN *see Foxhole Bay*

DILES LAKE 'Lake' is a Gower name for stream. Flows past *Coety Green*, appearing eventually on *Rhossili Bay*. Once a mill stream supporting three mills. **411912**

DRUIDS MOOR S. facing flanks of **Hardings Down**, below *Cathan*.
440900

DUNVANT [W. Dwfn-nant-Deep Stream]. Village and suburb of Swansea. Formerly a busy minor industrial centre with coalmines and brickworks, all now silent. Valley was cut by overflowing of ponded meltwater at the close of the Ice Age. Combined cycle and footpath uses route of former railway line through *Clyne Valley*. At the site of the former Dunvant Railway station stands a memorial to miners killed at the nearby Killan Colliery.

FPs to coast at *Blackpill* and inland to *Three Crosses*. **593937**

DYKE (THE) *see Groose (The)*

EYNON'S FORD Old Gower settlement on northern edge of Penrice Woods, near an old crossing of Penrice Stream. 200 yds. S. of main road (A4118), by lane alongside Reynoldston Police Station. Said to be named after George ap Eynon of Brynfield, Reynoldston in 17th cent., but name is recorded earlier.

One legend tells how a swarm of thousands of *very* (fairy) folk came one night to the farm, slaughtered an ox in the very sight of the farmer, skinned it, then sat down to a feast and ate it all up except, of course, for the bones. They then proceeded to fit it together again, so that the whole ox was restored except for one tiny leg bone. They hunted for this in great agitation, but in vain. From that day on, the ox was no worse for it, except for a slight limp on that leg!   **488887**

FAIRWOOD COMMON First Gower open space on main road out from Swansea, via Sketty and Killay. At *Upper Killay* (5m W. of Swansea) built-up area suddenly gives way to open moorland and long views of Gower and *Cefn Bryn*. Road forks here to form two main routes into the peninsula, South Road (A4118), to *Port-Eynon*, *Rhossili* and bays on south coastline; North Road (B4271), to *Llangennith* and North Gower villages. Both roads end in cul-de-sacs at the coast and there are few links between them. Tradition has it that the route of the south road was established by a farmer driving an ox plough across the common from a turn at Vennaway Lane, near *Kilvrough*, on the original road and then up to join the north road at *Upper Killay*.

Fairwood Lodge, once called 'Killay Lodge' is a mainly Georgian house which has been the residence of the Principal of University College, now University of Wales, Swansea and also the Judges' Lodgings for the Court of Assize in Swansea.

For two miles, Fairwood Common lies between the two roads, with *Swansea Airport* located here.   **552914 – 581926**

FAIRYHILL Lies among the narrow sunken lanes alongside the **Burry Pill**, at the W. end of *Cefn Bryn* and near to *Burry Green*.

One of Gower's few large country houses, much restored in recent years and now an award-winning hotel and restaurant. Once a fine residence, formerly owned by the Lucas and the Benson families. Lady Barham lived here in 1814 and she was instrumental in establishing six Calvinistic Methodist chapels in Gower.   **467912**

FALL BAY (NT) Secluded sandy bay near *Rhossili*, in shelter of limestone cliffs and *Tears Point*, and separated from Mewslade Bay by the NT headland of *Jacky's Tor*. Accessible, on foot only, from *Middleton* (1m), around headland from *Rhossili* (2m) or across sands at low water on spring tides from *Mewslade Bay* (½m E.). Boating, sands, cliff walks, fishing.

Fine exposure of Pleistocene raised beach. Good fossils in limestone on west side of bay. Iron Age promontory fort on *Lewes Castle*, magnificent cliff E. of bay.   **413874**

FORESTER'S CAVE *see Foxhole*

FOXHOLE Small rocky bay in Pennard Cliffs, a little E. of NT car park at *Southgate*. Track to *Minchin Hole* (400 yds. E.) begins here.
Devil's Kitchen is a small bone cave to the west of Foxhole Bay of no known archaeological interest.
Forester's Cave is 300 yds. W. of Foxhole Bay and about 30ft. above sea level. The only find – a large rhinoceros bone – is now in SwM.   **553872**

FOXHOLE SLADE In Port-Eynon-Rhossili Cliffs. A stone-strewn valley leading down to *Paviland Caves*.   **429858**

FROG LANE *see Llanmadoc*

FROG MOOR At foot of W. slopes of *Cefn Bryn* (½m W. of *Reynoldston*). Open land, marshy in places, with views of West Gower. Crossed by road, *Reynoldston* to *Fairyhill*, and various tracks.
FPs to *Knelston* (½m S.), *Burry Green* (1m W.).   **469905**

GANDERSTREET Roadway from *Oxwich Green* to *Oxwich*, passing near to *Oxwich Castle*.   **496864**

GIANT'S GRAVE (or Parc le Breos Tomb *shown on map as 'Long Cairn'*). *See Long Cairn.*

GOWER HERITAGE CENTRE *see Parkmill*

GOWER'S LOAD *see Bryn Farm*

GOWERTON (Welsh: Tregŵyr). Also previously known as *Gwter Felen* or, when the railway came, as *Gower Road*). Large and busy industrial village and shopping centre at eastern end of N. coast road (B4295).   **590963**

GOWER WAY STONE (at *GR 523888*) Large boulder on eastern end of *Cefn Bryn* above *Penmaen*, placed to mark the route of the Gower Way (a Gower Society project for the Millennium) which crosses the Lordship of Gower from Penlle'r castell to Rhossili. A plaque on the stone was unveiled by HRH the Prince of Wales in July 1998 to inaugurate the Gower Way.
See also Cefn Bryn

GRAVES END On *Pwlldu Head*. At this spot is a grave, marked with stones but concealed by bracken in summer. About 80 people, drowned in the wreck of the *Caesar* in November 1760, are buried here. This was the only spot on the rocky headland where a large enough grave could have been dug. The point at which the ship struck is a recess between massive rocks known today as *Caesar's Hole*.   **572864**
See also High Pennard

GREAT TOR Spectacular spur of cliff formed by vertical limestone strata, separating *Three Cliff Bay* from the two mile sweep of *Oxwich Bay*. To the west, crowned with a stile on the footpath, is *Honey Tor* and also *Little Tor*.

Leather's Hole is a bone cave high up on Great Tor. Difficult access from above, via gap between two humps on headland. Remains in SwM.

Benrick is the prominent rock just off *Penmaen Burrows* E. of Great Tor. *See also Tor Bay*   **530877**

GREEN CWM *see Llethrid Cwm*

GROOSE (THE) W. end of Llanrhidian Marsh (NT) and much dissected by water channels. A sea wall was built over 200 years ago to reclaim the nearby Cwm Ivy Marsh. After the salt had leached away the resulting fresh water marsh was fenced off into fields. The sea wall, known locally as 'The Dyke', was breached and the area flooded in 1974; the wall was heightened in an attempt to prevent a recurrence.   **446944**

FP along top of sea wall.

GUZZLEHOLE (or Guthole). Cavern in *Bishopston Valley* where the underground stream can be seen and heard roaring along. The cavern lies about halfway down the valley.   **575884**

HAEL LANE (from Welsh: 'heol' – roadway). Lane joining East Cliff, Pennard with Hael Farm.   **560877**

HANGMAN'S CROSS Where a number of ancient tracks meet on the roadway from *Penrice* to *Moorcorner* (at 1m W. of Penrice). This roadway is believed to follow the route of an old road from *Rhossili* to *Oxwich*. Old Sheep Lane is now a bridleway to *Oxwich*. Probably a gibbet was once erected here, at least one body being buried in nearby Grave Lane. Moorhouse Lane is a bridleway to *Scurlage*, across what, until the 1680s, was a large common known as 'Porteinon Moor'.   **483867**

See also Merrysun, Bryn-sil, Beggar's Pit

HARDINGS DOWN Smallest of the group of three Old Red Sandstone hills in far west of peninsula.(The others being *Llanmadoc Hill* & *Rhossili Down*). Rises to 152m (500ft.) ¾m S.E. of *Llangennith*.

There are a number of Iron Age earthwork enclosures on the slopes of the hill. Several footpaths from Llangennith and from main road ¾m E. of village.   **437906**

HARESLADE Wooded slade or valley behind *Brandy Cove*. Lower Hareslade Farm on lane leading to main road at *Pyle Corner*. Upper Hareslade Farm is on high land above the valley.   **584877**

HAYES WOOD (Hayes = Gower word for enclosed field). On lower slopes of *Cefn Bryn*. Part of the woodland of *Penrice* to north of *Home Farm*. 496892

HEATHERSLADE Small rocky bay in Pennard Cliffs ¼m W. of *Foxhole Bay* and near NT car park at *Southgate*. The nearby house, of the same name, now an Old People's Home, was the childhood home of Vernon Watkins, poet and friend of Dylan Thomas. 549873

HELWICK BANK *also HELWICK SANDS, see Port-Eynon*

HERONSTREET Roadway leading from *Oxwich Green* to *Eastern Slade* (½m W) where lane continues down towards *Slade Bay* and *The Sands* on the western side of *Oxwich Point*. 490860

HIGH PENNARD 1. Easterly limit of Pennard Cliffs. Small settlement above slopes overlooking Pwlldu Bay. *Pwlldu Head* rises near here to 300ft. In 1760 survivors of the wreck of the *Caesar* made their way up to this lonely spot to raise the alarm.
See Graves End 570870
2. A promontory fort on cliff top, overlooking *Hunts Bay* (NT) 567866
FPs down to *Bishopston Valley* and *Pwlldu*.

HIGHWAY Two farms: Great Highway and Little Highway, on road between *Pennard Church* and *Southgate*. Said to be notorious in 18th cent. as smugglers' headquarters. *Smugglers' Lane* is a footpath near here leading down to *Bishopston Valley* and *Pwlldu*. 559884

HILLEND 1. House and farm at foot of northern end of *Rhossili Down*, S.W. of *Llangennith*. Access to *Rhossili Bay* by short walk across dunes. Two cannons at present mounted in private garden outside house are said to have come from a wrecked ship. They have been dated as pre-1700 and are not necessarily of the same national origin, but they are now too worn to be conclusively identified.
Large camping and caravan site. Surfing, parking, shop. 418909
FPs to *Rhossili* around foot of *Rhossili Down* and across top of hill.
2. Farm at western end of Cefn Bryn (1m N.W. of *Reynoldston*). Also Little Hillend nearby. 472910

HOLT'S FIELD *see Manselfield*

HOLY'S WASH Short stretch of coast between *Slade* and *Oxwich Point*. 495853

HOME FARM Farm of Penrice Castle, on main S. road (A4118), opposite west gates of Penrice Park. Attractive raised granary across road nearby (a listed Grade 2 building).   **495890**
See also Kittle Top

Home Farm Granary

HONEY TOR *see Great Tor*

HORSE CLIFF On coastal footpath *Port-Eynon-Rhossili*, to west of *Paviland Caves*. Seen from Rhossili side, rising above *the Knave*, this is one of the most striking cliffs in Gower, the dip of the limestone strata being almost vertical. This is the only point on the coast where no flatter rocks are uncovered at low water.
Iron Age promontory fort on W. of cliff top.   **435860**

HORTON Seaside village at eastern end of *Port-Eynon Bay*. Bus from Swansea stops at top of village. From here lanes descend 200 feet to sea level in ¼ mile.
Dunes, firm sands, canoeing, fishing, walking, no PH, holiday accommodation.
Inshore Lifeboat Station. The large buoys visible off shore mark where the 'Prince Ivanhoe' ran aground in 1981.
CP, PO, shops, toilets.
FPs from lower village to Port-Eynon (½m W.), Oxwich (4m E.).
Also old Gower tracks from top of village via *Hangman's Cross* to *Penrice* (2m W.), *Reynoldston* (4m N.W.).   **474857**

HUNTS BAY *see Deepslade*

ILSTON (from Welsh Llan Illtyd Gŵyr). Hamlet in wooded valley of Ilston stream (pop. 300). This is one of the most ancient sites in Gower and still one of the most tranquil. The former quarry nearby is a nature reserve.
St. Illtyd's Church is possibly the least known in the peninsula, and gives the visitor an impression of incredible antiquity. Part of the church was restored in 1998.
Hoard of 91 Roman coins found in quarry in 1933. Now at SwM. and NatMW.   **557903**
FPs to *Parkmill* on S. road (A4118).
Narrow metalled lanes to *Lunnon* (1m W.) and to N. road (B4271) near *Cartersford Bridge* (1m N.).

ILSTON CWM Delightful little valley of the Ilston stream, known as the Killy-Willy, probably because of its rapid, twisting course down to *Parkmill*, reaching the sea eventually at *Three Cliff Bay*. The name, said to be of Irish origin, has also been given to an area of woodland overlooking the site of the early Pre-Reformation chapel referred to later.

Church of St. Illtyd, Ilston

At Trinity Well, ¼m from Parkmill end, are foundations of first Baptist Church established in Wales (1649-1660) with a memorial to founder John Myles, once rector of **Ilston** and founder of the community of Swansea in Massachusetts, USA. Close by are traces of foundations of a Pre-Reformation chapel. **551891 – 556904**

FP to **Ilston** (1¼m N.) begins at gate on main S. road (A4118), alongside the former Parkmill School, now the West Glamorgan Guide Activity Centre.

ITALY *see Moorcorner*

JACKY'S TOR (NT) *see Fall Bay*

KEENMORE LANE *see Pitton Cross*

KENNEXSTONE Site of farmhouse built in 1610 (near junction of **Llanmadoc** road with main road to **Llangennith**) which was removed stone by stone to St. Fagans Museum of Welsh Life and re-erected there in 1963. **450916**

KILLAY (from Welsh: Cil, a refuge). Extensive residential area (pop. 4,742). PHs, petrol, shops, St. Hilary's Church, bowls, tennis. Main road dips steeply to cross Clyne Valley at the former LMS railway line, now a cycle/footpath to **Blackpill** and **Dunvant**. **Clyne Valley** is a Country Park, with access from **Killay**, **Dunvant** and **Blackpill**. Considerable quantities of war materials were brought along the railway track and into Swansea Docks in preparation for the D-day landings during World War II. Near the **Brick Pit**, a short distance south along the cycle/footpath, is a well preserved 'pillbox' originally built to guard the railway line.

See also Upper Killay **602929**

KILLY-WILLY *see Ilston Cwm*

KILVROUGH MANOR (Welsh, Cilfrew). (¼m S.W. of *Fairwood Common*) on main S. road (A4118). Imposing 18th cent. mansion in 2½ ha. (6 acres) of private grounds. Now used as an educational centre for young people.

Built by Rowland Dawkins in 1585, this is possibly the original manor house of *Langrove*. It was rebuilt in the 18th century. Until the late 19th century, the estate was run as a 'hunting estate', *see below*.

Early in the 19th century Mrs Green, the Asian widow of the owner Major Green, made it known that she intended to carry out the custom of her country and place herself, along with the body of her dead husband, on a funeral pyre and ordered a quantity of wood to be prepared for that purpose. However, after a great furore in the area, she eventually consented to a funeral at Pennard Church.

Later in the century, Thomas Penrice, the second owner of that name, set about developing the estate and built the high wall surrounding it, as a shelter for his kitchen gardens at the side of the road down to *Parkmill*. This same Thomas Penrice also built Parkmill School, various farms and encouraged the building of the Gower Inn on the site of the male workhouse (the corresponding female workhouse being at the other end of the village near to the present day '*Gower Heritage Centre*').

Langrove was formerly a substantial farm, part of the ancient manor already in existence in days of Edward II (14th cent.). Now motel and country club on S. road (A4118) across *Fairwood Common* are on site of a 19th century Keeper's Cottage.

Cannisland is a residential site of mobile homes nearby.

Vennaway Lane. (Part of the B4436 road). Name given to section of roadway linking A4118 road over *Fairwood Common* with the *Southgate* road near *Pennard* Church. This was part of a very early road from South Gower through *Bishopston* to *Blackpill*.

Near the A4118 junction is a well preserved example of one of the many Gower limekilns, reminders of what was once a major local activity. Also, at the junction, the grove of trees contains a Gower Society commemorative plaque.

A round tower in field W. of Kilvrough Manor is a folly with no public access, built by a former owner.   559893

KIMLEY MOOR Farm on B4247 road 1½m E. of *Rhossili*.   439875

KINGSHALL Farmhouse ruin at foot of eastern slopes of *Rhossili Down*. A green way (Kingshall Lane) leads towards *Llandewi* (2m E.). This may have been an ancient roadway opening on to the downs, with paths S. to *Rhossili* and N. to *Llangennith*. The open field between Kingshall and *Old Henllys* is called 'Furzy Whole Moor' recalling the name of a hamlet of four houses, *Whole Moor*, which once lay to the north of Kingshall Lane.

There is little to account for Kingshall's grand name, but it was once owned by a branch of the powerful Lucas family.

See Old Henllys   435892

KITCHEN CORNER Little, sheltered inlet under former coastguard lookout station at *Rhossili*, immediately at E. tip of *Rhossili Bay*. Quarrying in the last century has left its mark all along this headland. Limestone used to be shipped from these 'flotquars' to Somerset and Devon. The winch of a former quarry and an early 20th century boathouse are still in place.   **402875**

Kitchen Corner

KITHEN WELL (*sometimes* '*Kitchen Well*') One of the ancient wells of Gower, it is actually a spring as are many of the Gower 'wells'. In the hollow alongside the road to the forestry car park at *Green Cwm*.   **539886**

KITTLE (?Kyte Hill) Pop. 569. On W. side of *Bishopston Valley* (NT). Housing development with remnants of small village green, a junction of roads leading to *Parkmill* and to *Fairwood Common*. Shops. PH. The old main road descends sharply and turns up again over a ford near *Bishopston* church; this road is now best covered on foot. The modern road to Parkmill (B4436) follows a less steep course but has a wide sweeping bend beside Barland Quarry.

Kittle Hill Lane runs towards Fairwood Common and passes the large Stonegate Poultry Farm. *See Barland Common.*   **574893**

KITTLE TOP (or Kettle Top). Huge rounded grassy mound alongside main S. road (A4118), 200 yds. W. of Penrice *Home Farm*, possibly of glacial origin. The site is crossed by a FP between *Reynoldston and Millwood*.
   493888

KNAB (THE), also known as '*Knab Rock*'. Slipway at *Southend, Oystermouth*. On coastal footpath/cycleway, also footpath to *Mumbles Hill*.

CP, PH, cafe, toilets.   **626876**

KNAVE, THE Remarkable conical rock, dominating inlet W. of *Horse Cliff* and ¼m W. of *Paviland Caves*. Smaller rocks on seaward side known as the Bull and Calf.   **432862**

KNELSTON (Knoyle's Farm). Small settlement (pop. 193) of some antiquity on a conspicuous rise on main road, (A4118) 1m S.W. of *Reynoldston*. Shop, petrol, small caravan site.

Ruins of church of St. Taurin (12th cent.) in field behind present school. Later known as Llan y Tair Mair (Church of the Three Marys). It was already in ruins in 17th cent.

Three fine standing stones near here; one, *The Knelston Stone*, a little N. of above ruin; the other two, *Burry Eastern* and *Burry Western Stones*, are 1m. to N.W. *Trumpet Lane* is an old Gower lane between Knelston and *Burry Head*. Central section is not open, but a public right of way on foot runs alongside lane.   **467890**

FPs to *Burry* (2m N.) and to *Berry* (1m S.).

See also Stouthall

LAGADRANTA (Welsh: 'llygad rhandir' – source at foot of slope). Large caravan park. Former farm overlooking **Broughton Bay**. One legend tells how the wife of the farmer here lent a sieve to a little old woman, who in gratitude to her, said her beer cask would never run dry, provided she told no one about this. She couldn't keep the secret, so there was no endless supply of beer.   **428930**

LANDIMORE North Gower hamlet descending steeply to the salt marshes 1m E. of **Cheriton**. Once a small port and a weaving village. Traces of castle (also known as **Bovehill Castle**) on slopes of hill W.; turn seawards off **Oldwalls-Cheriton** road.   **465931**
See also Groose, Loughor Estuary

LANGLAND BAY (Long Land, a reference to the former strip fields). Popular beach, within a short distance of Swansea, patrolled in summer by lifeguards. Largely unspoilt, in a picturesque setting. The beach huts are a unique feature; these are day huts, leased for the season from the local council. Good sands, boating, walking, with excellent coastal views from cliffs in each direction. The romantic-looking mock-Gothic building overlooking the beach was built as a summer villa for Henry Crawshay, son of the Merthyr iron-master, Richard Crawshay. Formerly called 'Llan-y-llan' (*the name is apparently meaningless*) and later known as Langland Castle, it was enlarged to become the Langland Castle Hotel and then the original Langland Bay Hotel. It is now a convalescent home. The later Langland Bay Hotel was built from the original coachman's house and outbuildings and the site is now occupied by the apartments 'Crawshay Court'.

The 'Hole in the Wall' shop in the middle of the bay once housed the water pump used in the supply of sea water to the hotel for salt water baths.

The eastern end of the bay is known as '*Rotherslade*' or, sometimes, as '*Little Langland*', which can be reached on foot along the promenade from **Langland Bay** or by road from Langland Corner on the **Oystermouth** to **Caswell** road. A very deteriorated reinforced concrete structure which formerly housed a cafe, dance hall and sun deck has been replaced by a series of landscaped terraces and steps which lead down to the bay.

Fine cliff walks to **Mumbles Pier**, via **Limeslade** (1½m E.) and to **Caswell** (1½m W.).

Surfing, guest houses, car park, beach huts, tennis courts, refreshments, toilets, golf course (18), telephone, hotel (at Rotherslade).   **607874**

LANGROVE *see Kilvrough Manor*

LEASON Small hamlet in North Gower, once a centre of weaving.
FPs to **Weobley Castle** (1½m W.) and along edge of salt marshes to **Landimore** (1m E.).   **483925**

LEATHER'S HOLE *see Great Tor*

LEWES CASTLE *see Fall Bay*

LIMESLADE BAY Sheltered pebble beach, some sand when tide out; small inlet ½m W. of Mumbles Head. There are many *'slades'* – a Gower name given to a green, often gorse-covered, usually dry, limestone valley opening out to the sea.

Walled-in entrance to old iron ore working (worked perhaps even by the Romans) can be seen at head of bay.

Many housing developments, especially in *Plunch Lane,* which leads to *Mare's Pool* and *Thistleboon.*

Car park above **Bracelet Bay**. Refreshments. Holiday accommodation at *Plunch Lane.* **626871**

Cliff walk to **Langland** (1½m W.). Past **Tutt Point** to **Mumbles Pier** (1m E.) Walks inland around **Mumbles Hill** with good views.

LITTLE REYNOLDSTON Small hamlet on left of minor road leading to **Reynoldston** village just off A4118. The former farm of Little Reynoldston originally dates from the late 1500s or early 1600s. The farmhouse is now a private residence and most of the yard and outbuildings are used by the National Trust as their Gower depot and offices. **489893**

LLANDEWI (Church of St. Dewi). Ancient settlement (pop. 26) with church and manor house, ½m W. of **Knelston**, 1½m S.W. of **Reynoldston**, a little along **Burry Lane**. Seen from rise of Knelston, the church and few farm buildings stand out against the hills of West Gower and we get some idea of the significance of this little spot as a link between the north and south of the peninsula.

In medieval times a number of family seats were concentrated here: Scurlage, Old Henllys, Brynfield, also Kingshall.

Church of St. Dewi, Llandewi

The Church of St. Dewi is probably the least symmetrical in the peninsula but has dignity and charm.

Manor House, opposite church, built by Mansel family in 16th cent., near site of a Bishop's Palace. Lived in by Mansel family. The Palace walls form part of present farmhouse. **460891**

See also Old Henllys, Scurlage, Kingshall, Burry

LLANGENNITH (Church of St. Cenydd). End point of N. road – B4295 – (16m to Swansea). Hotel, PH, PO, guest houses, refreshments, caravan sites (pop. 350). Not a seaside village, but several bays within short distance, and its very situation, lying where lower slopes of three hills meet (*Llanmadoc Hill, Rhossili Down* and *Hardings Down*), has always made the sea the focal point of village life. Any wreck, or smuggling exploit, and 'Llangenny' folk were there as quickly as anyone. In fact, this must have been one of the liveliest villages in Gower at one time, with a thriving weaving industry and stories of cockfighting, gaming, prize-fighting, wedding sprees, harvest dances and 'stepping' are still told with relish. One anecdote will illustrate the independence of mind and the former remoteness of life in Gower: when the Government decided to introduce daylight saving during the First World War, there was a public meeting held in North Gower to discuss whether *they* would put their clocks on; they eventually decided solemnly they would give it a trial for a month!

Church of St. Cenydd, Llangennith

St. Cenydd's Church is the largest in Gower and is believed to have grown from the church of Llangennith Priory, founded in the 6th century by the Celtic St. Cenydd.

Adjoining church, on lane to **Coety Green** is *College Farm*. The Priory of St. Cenydd in 1441 became the property of All Souls College, Oxford, which owned it until 1838.

Opposite lych gate on green is ancient village well, restored in 1998, with faint traces of early cross cut into its stone cover.   **426915**

FPs to **Rhossili Sands** (1m W.): **Broughton Bay** (1m N.); **Bluepool Bay** (1½m N.W.): and across hills to **Rhossili** (3m S.), **Llanmadoc** (1½m N.E.).

See also Hillend

LLANMADOC (Church of St. Madoc). North Gower village (pop. 156), overlooking the **Burry Estuary**, on the slopes of **Llanmadoc Hill**.

27

Church of St. Madog, Llanmadog

Not a coastal village but access to sea and sands to W. and salt marshes to N. Mostly strung out along *Rattle Street* and descending past *Frog Lane* towards **Cheriton**. Frog Lane, which is now a track leading towards *The Groose* was once a hamlet off main road as it descends in the direction of **Cheriton**.

For many years a Christian Youth Holiday Camp has existed here. Once a lively weaving centre; some of the reconstructed woollen factory in St. Fagans came from here. A house called 'The Factory' is a reminder of the trade.

The Church of St. Madoc is reputed to have been founded in the 6th century.

PO, PH, shop, guest houses, refreshments, caravan site.　　　**440934**
See also Cwm Ivy, Spritsail Tor, Lagadranta

LLANMADOC HILL At 186m. (610ft.) one of the highest points in Gower, formed of Old Red Sandstone, a landmark in West Gower: also known as *Llanmadoc Down*. Some fine views from the top and from the approaches down to village. At E. end earthworks known as **The Bulwark**, also some Bronze Age cairns. Fragments of cinerary urn in SwM.　　　**430924**

FPs, and lanes to **Broughton Bay** (1m W.), **Whiteford Burrows** (½m N.W.) and across hill to **Llangennith** (1½m S.W.).

LLANMORLAIS (from Welsh 'Glanmorlais' – on the banks of the Morlais stream). A mixed village (pop. 1,047) of 19th century miners' cottages, farms, Tirzah Baptist chapel, and more modern housing. Once the terminus of the railway from **Gowerton** and was a centre of considerable mining activity. Now connected with the cockling industry at nearby **Crofty**.　　　**529947**

LLANRHIDIAN North Gower estuarine village (pop. 431) sloping sharply down to the salt marshes. Approach road at junction of N. road from *Cillibion* (B4295) and road from *Penclawdd* (4m to N.E.) – B4271. Once a centre of family weaving and sheep rearing. Character of old village not entirely altered in spite of new buildings. The North Gower Hotel is situated on the road to Cillibion, just outside the village.

The Church of St. Illtyd and St. Rhidian is situated beneath a limestone bluff, and its massive western tower is dwarfed only by the neighbouring cliff.

A grotesquely carved stone may be seen in the porch. Known as 'The Leper Stone', it is a massive block of stone, bearing simple representations of human figures and animals carved on one face. It was dug up in the churchyard in the 19th cent., and was moved to the protection of the porch about 1910. It is believed to date from the 9th cent. A.D.

A standing stone (conglomerate) mounted on a limestone base on the green may be the remains of the village cross, and is said to have been used as a sort of pillory before the 19th century; it was re-erected in 1821 by the villagers, who erected its limestone partner in 1844.

Church of St. Illtyd and St. Rhidian, Llanrhidian

Butter Well is an ancient well in a private garden near Llanrhidian Church. From 1185 there are legends that a copious stream of milk and butterfat issued from it. Known also as St. Illtyd's Well.

There were formerly two mills on the tiny stream which runs through Llanrhidian; now only Nether Mill remains. The iron wheel had gone by the 1960s, but the Mill building, on three floors, with an attractive mill pond alongside, is of interest. A tablet below the large stone chimney indicates that the year of building was 1803.

Petrol, PH/restaurant, TIC.   **497923**

FPs below cliffs to **Weobley Castle** (1¼m W.), along salt marshes to **Llanmorlais** (3m E.). Once the main road.

See Cil Ifor Top

LLETHRID Small sheltered farming settlement on N. road, B4271, at W. limit of **Pengwern Common**, 4½m W. of **Upper Killay**. Here the road twists and descends steeply into a little wooded valley to cross the upper stream of the Parkmill Pill, before the stream enters **Green Cwm** and disappears for part of the way underground.

Near the old lodge house of the former Parc le Breos estate, beside the bridge, is the entrance (now sealed) to *Llethrid Swallet*, on private land. This is a large limestone cave with a wealth of stalagmites and stalactites, some of rare mud formations. The fragile calcite deposits and mud formations are amongst the few recorded in Britain.   **530913**

FP to **Green Cwm** and **Parkmill** near bridge on S. and to **Cillibion** N.

LLETHRID CWM, or *Parc le Breos valley*. An alternative name for *Green Cwm;* which is a delightful wooded valley, two miles long, stretching from **Parkmill** northwards to **Llethrid**. A public footpath runs through the valley, passing near **Cathole Cave**, the **Giant's Grave** and a restored lime-kiln near an old quarry. The valley is formed in limestone; its stream now runs underground from Llethrid, and is thought to reappear at the water pumping station at the Parkmill end of the valley near the car park.

See also Tor Bay   **530913 – 538896**

LLWYN Y BWCH Old farm to S. of **Old Walls**. Once associated with the Gordon family, an ancient family of **Weobley Castle** and N.W. Gower.

                    484916

LONG CAIRN (Parkmill) Megalithic tomb in Green Cwm (¾m N. of Parkmill). Well preserved chambered long barrow (approx. 3500 BC). Restored by the former Ministry of Works. Remains of about two dozen human beings found in 1869. Probably built originally on bank of stream, now flowing underground. For access, *see Cathole* (1). Remains in Ashmolean Museum.

See also Giant's Grave   **537898**

LONGHOLE CAVE Bone cave high on Overton Cliff, 1m W. of *Port-eynon Point*. Reached by a rough track from above or below. Take FP above rocks from *Overton Mere* or follow Overton Lane to end, then stone wall for 400 yards, descend slade towards the cave about 130ft. above HWM.
Considerable animal remains and implements in SwM and BM. **451850**

LOUGHOR, RIVER also **LOUGHOR ESTUARY** (also known as the *Burry Estuary*). Gower is bounded on its N. side by the estuary of the Loughor River, a river which drains approx. 250 sq. miles of the surrounding area. The flats and marshes formed by the River Loughor after it has been joined by the Dulais and by the combined Llan & Lliw, that descend from the hills to the north, are rich in flora and wild life and offer a complete contrast to the cliffs and bays of the peninsula's south coast. This is a major location for wading birds and the marshes are utilized mainly for grazing by semi wild ponies where formerly there were sheep and cattle.
See also Groose (The), Penclawdd, Crofty

LUCAS BAY *see Oxwich Point*

LUNNON (Welsh: Llwyn-onn – ash grove). Hamlet above *Parkmill*, linked by lane with *Ilston* (¾m N.E.). Approach road, continuing to *Pen-gwern Common*, leaves A4118 road at *Parkmill* and ascends hill sharply. This is only road link between B4271 and A4118 roads from *Killay* as far as *Reynoldston*. . **546897**

MANSELFIELD Formerly a separate hamlet now an eastern continuation of *Murton* towards *Newton*.
Nearby *Holt's Field* is a community which has developed from one of the many chalet sites built in the area between the two World Wars. **585890**

MANSELFOLD Farm in N. Gower. The close association of the Mansel family with Gower is recalled by several place names.
The Mansel family, one of the ancient families of Britain, arrived with William the Conqueror (name derives from Le Mans). It has had connections with Gower ever since. For complete pedigree of family see J. D. Davies's *History of West Gower*. Among famous members of the family was Sir John Mansel, who was Lord Chancellor to Henry III (13th cent.). **475919**

MANSEL JACK *see Samson's Jack*

MARGAM FARM At the western end of lane – known as Margam Lane – which leaves main Porteynon road at *Moorcorner*, i.e. at junction with road to *Horton*. The often muddy track, which has a turning to *Overton* half way along it, emerges onto the main *Rhossili* road at Margam Corner,

¼m E. of **Pyle Well**. For walkers only, it is a short cut between the villages. Tradition that this is part of very old drovers road into Swansea, via **Penrice**.

Name recalls direct connection between the Mansels of Penrice and Margam Castle, near Port Talbot, which eventually became their home.   **454867**

MAYALS Now a suburb of Swansea at the western edge of **Clyne Common**. Formerly known as Le Mayals. Mayals Road runs alongside the municipal park of Clyne Gardens with its extensive collection of rhododendrons and large bog garden.

See also Blackpill   **608903**

MERRYSUN Name of former farmhouse, now renovated, near Horton. Also, a section of Penrice parish. Possibly named after an ancient inn which stood near here. Often associated with the name *Cold Comfort*.   **477872**

MEWSLADE BAY (?from mew = seagull). (NT & SSSI). One of the smaller bays near **Rhossili**, immediately W. of **Thurba Head**. Spectacular rock scenery. Good sands, completely covered for two or three hours around HW. Reached by a moderate walk down typical Gower slade.

In a small quarry on W. side of valley bones of six or seven humans found in last century. On opposite side, nearer the sea and 120 feet up, the small Mewslade Cave can be seen. Some signs of human habitation, remains in SwM.

The Valley is partly-owned by the NT. Access is by footpath from CP and bus stop at **Pitton**.

Cliff FP **Port-Eynon-Rhossili** skirts bay.   **421873**

MIDDLETON One of sections of Rhossili parish (½m E. of church), and centre of its life in some ways with its village hall. There used to be three inns in Middleton, but now there are none. The last one, the Ship Inn, is now Ship Farm, next to the village hall. The area has connections with Edgar Evans who was born in a cottage in School Lane and who died on Scott's last expedition to the South Pole. There is a memorial in Rhossili church. Bus stop, telephone, limited parking in hall CP.

Footpaths to **Fall Bay**, to **Mewslade**, and path across **Rhossili Down** to **Llangennith** (3m N.).   **424877**

MILL WOOD An article in *Gower* in 1959 contained the statement '. . . Mill Wood is gone. Where it stood there is a bald and scarred hillside in the heart of Gower . . .' Fortunately the woodland has regrown in the interveening years and we can again enjoy the many pleasant walks to places such as Bryn-sil Top and the vanished hamlet of Capon's Hill. The old mill pond and mill leat can be examined as well as the ruin of the mill building and the ponds, which were part of an early fish farming operation. The mill ruin stands at the bottom of Penny Hitch, where tradition has it that horses, with hire charge of one penny, used to be kept here to help carts up steep hill.   **490882**

See also Penrice

Llandewi Church   H.E.G.

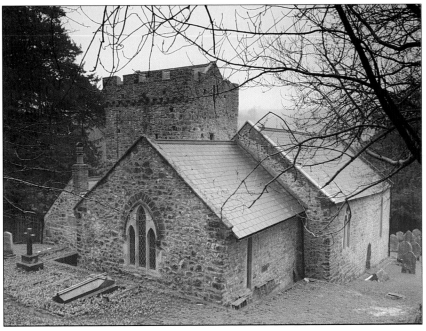

St. Illtyd Church, Ilston   H.E.G.

Marsh Fritillary, Welshmoor   *H.E.G.*

Broad Pool, Cefn Bryn Common   *H.E.G.*

Spring Squill, Worms Head   H.E.G.

Yellow Whitlow Grass, Overton   H.E.G.

Mewslade Bay

H.E.G.

MINCHIN HOLE The largest of the coastal caves and a SSSI, situated in the cliff face 600 yards SSE. of the *Southgate* bus terminus, below a small but prominent limestone knoll. The cave has been extensively excavated in recent years, and has produced remains of elephant, bison, soft-nosed rhinoceros and hyena, as well as traces of human occupation in more recent times. Accessible with care and some scrambling. Remains in SwM. **555867**

MONKSLAND Farm near *Scurlage* **459877**

MOORCORNER At junction of main *Port-Eynon* road with road to *Horton* and *Penrice*. This is E. end of Margam Lane and beginning of FP to *Rhossili*. The name recalls the long vanished '*Porteinon Moor*', which stretched for almost a mile N. and E. of this spot. The open moorland was enclosed piecemeal by neighbouring farmers between 1680 and 1690. The main road between Moorcorner and Scurlage was sometimes known as '*Italy*'. **464865**
See also Margam

MOORMILLS A large sink hole on *Cefn Bryn* NW of *Broad Pool*. Formed by the collapse of land into a cavern in the underlying limestone. Although several streams empty into it Moormills is a dry sinkhole. **506913**
See also Broad Pool

MOUNT HERMON *see Penclawdd*

MOUNTYBANK *see Penrice*

MUMBLES (?from Fr. mamelles = breasts). Prominent twin limestone islets marking western extremity of Swansea Bay. Both acccessible at low water, but watch the tide! On the outer islet are the lighthouse, built in 1793, and a coast defence fort of 1861. Mumbles Pier is nearby, from which the Lifeboat House is reached. Usually the name is given to the whole of this end of Swansea Bay, including *Oystermouth* and *Southend*. At the Pier, a

Mumbles Pier (1965)

car park now occupies the site of the terminus of the former Mumbles Railway, the first in the world to carry passengers, and which was closed in 1960. The railway ran to Swansea along the coast as far as **Blackpill** and then on the landward side of the golf course and alongside the Mumbles Road as far as the vicinity of the present St. David's Car Park. A promenade now follows the trackbed as far as Blackpill sharing the space with a cycleway from Southend onwards. After Blackpill the combined pathway continues along the trackbed of the former LMS line into Swansea so providing a continuous route around the bay.

In the 1870s, the outer island was the scene of very early experiments in overwater telegraphy conducted by J. D. Llewelyn of Penllergare and Professor Sir Charles Wheatstone, which anticipated by many years Marconi's experiments with radio further up the Bristol Channel.

Car parks, cafes, amusements, PHs, Mumbles Rowing Club. Two Lifeboats.   **635871**
See also Southend, Oystermouth

MUMBLES HILL High ground behind **Bracelet Bay**, site of many anti-aircraft installations during World War II and now a Nature Reserve with views over Swansea Bay and the Bristol Channel. A radio station is still in use on the hill.   **627873**
See also Knab Rock

MURTON (pop. 1138) Now part of **Bishopston**, with a village green and well. Farm (plant nursery) and some old cottages remain, but many new developments. The Methodist chapel was extended in 1998. The village has both a community and chapel hall. Once a centre for market gardening. Bus stop, PO, PH, shop. Approach road at W. end of **Clyne Common** off B4436, otherwise through Bishopston (½m W.) along narrow lane.   **588890**

MYNYDD BACH Y COCS (Welsh: 'cocos' = cockles). Small hill, source of Morlais river on common land south-west of **Three Crosses**. The remains of Whitewalls Colliery, which operated until 1948, can be seen at the eastern end of the common. The ruin of Carmel Chapel (1889) lies beside the road near the western end. Many footpaths radiate from the common towards **Three Crosses**, **Blue Anchor** and **Gelli Hir**.   **558935**

NEWTON 1. (pop. 2,960) Formerly a separate village community, now virtually joined to **Oystermouth**. Enlarged by recent development, but with much of its basic street plan and character remaining. The village once stood in the centre of an area of long, narrow fields derived from the enclosed strips of an early medieval open field settlement. The chancel of St. Peter's church contains a memorial tablet to hymn writer Francis Ridley Havergal, who helped teach at nearby Paraclete, originally one of Lady Barnham's chapels (see *Fairyhill*). PH.   **603882**
See also Caswell

2. Farm ruin near **Pilton Green**. As early as 1840 Newton Farm was being worked with Pilton Green and is now split between **Margam Farm** and Great Pitton Farm near **Rhossili**.   452880

NICHOLASTON Coastal strip between **Cefn Bryn** and the sea, reaching to about 1m W. of **Penmaen**, each side of the A4118 road (pop. 90). The houses, scattered farms, and a few guest houses, enjoy a variety of landscape probably unrivalled in Gower: On the seaward side, Nicholaston Woods, **Three Cliff Bay** plus much of **Oxwich Bay**, and behind, the slopes of **Cefn Bryn**.

Camping, caravan park, garden centre and pick your own fruit.

Eastern end of Nicholaston Woods is also known as *Crawley Woods* a few minutes' walk from Nicholaston Cross (½m W. of Penmaen) down towards sea and **Oxwich Bay**. Unusual combination of beach, cliff, dune and woodland. There is an Iron Age promontory fort on the small headland overlooking burrows and the sharp finger of rock known as *Crawley Point*, near the footpath, high up at edge of *Crawley Woods*, marks an excellent view point above **Oxwich Bay**.

The Church of St. Nicholas stands isolated from rest of its parish, on a busy winding stretch of the A4118.   523884

NORTH HILL TOR (known locally as *Nottle Tor*). Prominent limestone headland overlooking marshes of the **Burry Estuary** ½m N. of **Cheriton**. The massive earthwork on private land here may be of Norman date. 453937

NORTHWAY Part of **Bishopston** at western limit of **Clyne Common** and near junction of the road to **Murton**.

Petrol.   585894

NORTON 1. Former hamlet off Mumbles Road N.W. of **Oystermouth**, now swallowed up in urban development. The neo-classical Norton House is, at present, a restaurant and hotel.   614886

2. Farm high over **Oxwich** Bay, on lane joining Oxwich Castle with **Penrice**. Norman (?) earthwork here.   492865

NOTT HILL (NT) Small but prominent hill overlooking **Three Cliff Bay** on W. side. Superb views over this bay. Accessible by lane (the former Parish Road) from green on top of Penmaen Hill.   535885

NOTTLE TOR *see North Hill Tor*

OLD HENLLYS (Welsh: Hen llys = old court). Locally known as *Henllis*. A remote farmhouse 1m W. of **Llandewi**, along the wide, green Kingshall Lane. Once a manor house, seat of the Mansel family. Much of the old walling can still be seen. Outside chimney typical of old Gower houses. Behind house, capacious cellars, said to have been built by Mansels for concealing contraband goods. An underground passage is said to have linked these cellars with **Rhossili** (over two miles away!).

In fields beside the lane from Old Henllys to **Llandewi** the ruins of small lime kilns and quarries can be seen. Many farms produced their own lime to use to reduce soil acidity. Marl was also dug here. Marl is a clay material rich in lime which was also used as a soil improver.

FPs. to **Hardings Down** (1m N.W.); to **Pilton Green**. Lane continues W. to the ruin of **Kingshall** farm (lm W.) and **Rhossili Down**.   447890

OLD SHEEP LANE *see Hangman's Cross*

OLDWALLS Hamlet 1m W. of Llanrhidian. PH. Two standing stones in fields nearby. Ebenezer Presbyterian Chapel was originally a Wesleyan building.   488919

FPs **Leason** (½m) and **Llanrhidian** (½m) N.; **Cefn Bryn** (¾m) S.

OVERTON (*a farm on a bank* – from OE '*offer*' and '*tun*'). Secluded part of **Porteynon** to W. and overlooking village. Lane turns off main road near top of Porteynon Hill (¼m from village). No through road for cars, but FP continues on to cliffs for **Paviland** and **Rhossili**. Nearest access to sea (on foot) is at far end of hamlet, by lane to **Overton Mere**.   462853

OVERTON MERE (NT) Sheltered pebbly beach W. of Porteynon Point. Bathing not easy. Reached by track around **Port-Eynon Point**, and FP opposite PO at **Port-Eynon**, or by lane from **Overton**.   464848
See Culver Hole

OXWICH (variously attributed to Scand. ax = water, wick = creek or wich = salt or wic = farm). Small seaside village (pop. 172) of some antiquity, along lanes at W. end of a magnificent three mile sweep of sands. Guest houses, shops, refreshments, PO, hotel/restaurant, bar, caravan parks, coastguard. Once small port exporting limestone. Two castles nearby. A community, largely by-passed by the heavy holiday traffic to the bay. There are many picturesque cottages in traditional Gower style. In the 18th cent. John Wesley stayed in one of these cottages during his visits to the area. The 'Wesley' cottage can be seen on the right about 100yds from junction with the marsh road.

One of the charms of the *Church of St. Illtyd* lies in its site, half-hidden by trees on the hillside by the sea.   499865

OXWICH BAY A large, privately owned, car park, right on the beach, dominates the approach. Its accessibility makes it, with **Porteynon**, one of the most popular beaches for boating. There is a vast curving expanse of sand, with a rich and colourful background of sand dunes, salt marshes, woodland, with cliffs at each end and **Cefn Bryn** in the background. These provide a variety of plant and bird life rarely found in Britain. Use special care towards all wild life here: this is a National Nature Reserve. Nature trail leaflets are available.

The large old building on the foreshore is the 'Coal House' which was used in the past to store coal delivered into the bay by sea. Slight traces of the 'Coal Road' can still be seen together with the route taken by bathing machines from Penrice House.

FPs around Oxwich Point to *Horton* (4m W.), *Porteynon* (4½m W.) via *Slade* (3m W.).

Lanes through village to *Penrice* (1½m), thence to Horton (3½m). Another through *Oxwich Green* to Slade (1m). Walks across sands or dunes to *Crawley Woods* and *Tor Bay*.

Best approach to Oxwich is a steep narrow road from *The Towers* on main A4118 road; the beginning was an ancient sunken lane on E. Side of Penrice Park, which then crossed marshes and meres (1½m in all). During World War II the road (known locally as 'The American Road' was 'improved' to allow access to the beach for military vehicles which also resulted in a large area of the dunes being flattened.

The original salt marshes were drained in the 19th century to provide farm land in a much praised enterprise. However, lack of manpower during wartime resulted in the neglect of the drainage system which can still be seen today.

OXWICH CASTLE (charge) 16th century fortified manor house, open to the public, charge. Restored and under the care of CADW. Not visible from village, but with fine views over the bay towards *Pwlldu* Head.
4978863

Pigeon House, Oxwich Castle

OXWICH GREEN Little wind-swept settlement, part of *Oxwich* and 1m to W. A few guest houses and two caravan parks. At top of steep hill that leaves Oxwich near to beach, passes Oxwich Castle and along what is known as Ganderstreet. The road continues through Oxwich Green to *Slade*.

FPs to Oxwich, *Horton* and *Hangman's Cross*. **495860**

OXWICH POINT The second highest headland in Gower at 85m. (250ft.); protects *Oxwich Bay* from the southwesterlies, but the remains of some of the many wrecks may still be seen on its weather side.

Lucas Bay, a small shingle bay between *Holy's Wash* and *Oxwich Point*. **513850**

OYSTERMOUTH (also known as '*Mumbles*') name said to derived from Welsh 'Ystumllwynarth' and was recorded as 'Ostreme' in 1284. (pop. 3,595). Sailing and water ski-ing centre at nearby *Knab Rock, Southend*. Hotels, shops, cafes many pubs and guest houses. Older parts of village straggle up the steep limestone cliffs, and were built when quarrying, iron ore working and oyster fishing were thriving occupations here.

The Church of All Saints is said to have been built on the site of a Roman villa. The three bells in the church tower, which bear inscription in Spanish dating from the 18th and early 19th centuries, are reputed to have been brought from the gutted cathedral of Santiago de Cuba by one of the Swansea copper ore barques and were presented to the church in about 1865 by Mr Aubrey Vivian.

Oystermouth castle dominates the view here. Entertainments are held in holiday season with the castle as backdrop. PHs, PO, shops, TIC, CPs on seafront and in quarry.   **616882**
See also Tor Bay

PARC LE BREOS A secluded country house, 1m W. of *Parkmill*. It stands surrounded by Parc Woods and takes its name from the private hunting ground of the Norman family of de Breos, which held the Lordship of Gower in the 13th and 14th centuries. The course of this old park boundary bank can be traced for nearly 6 miles. Later, in the 19th century, the park became part of the hunting grounds for the Vivians.

A grove of trees in Parc Woods was planted for the Golden Jubilee of the Gower Society in 1998.   **545892**
See Green Cwm, Penclawdd

PARKMILL (mentioned in 1583). Here the A4118 runs in a steep-sided narrow wooded valley and the village of Parkmill lines the road from the mock-Gothic former school house to the Park Mill itself ½m to W. The school is now the West Glamorgan Guides' Activity Centre and the mill, an ancient, restored water mill, is now the centrepiece of the *Gower Heritage Centre*. Another change is that Mount Pisgah, established by Lady Barham (see *Fairyhill*), is also now the P.O. premises. Shops TIC, PO, PH, petrol, CPs (one is summer only).

Stonemill is the eastern end of Parkmill, near Guides' Activity Centre, the former school, and the Gower Inn.
See also Kilvrough Manor.   **544893**
FP's and bridleways to *Penmaen, Ilston, Three Cliff Bay*.

PAVILAND Also known as *Paviland Manor*. Isolated farm, 2m E. of *Rhossili*, lying between A4118 and sea. Entrance gate a few yards E. of *Pyle Well*. FP to cliffs and *Paviland Caves* along W. edge of farmland, not by gate, but by stile marked by fingerpost on main road 150 yds nearer Rhossili at *Pilton Green*.   **448865**

PAVILAND CAVES Two caves in remote cliff face 2m W. of *Port-Eynon* and S. of *Paviland Farm*.

1. *Goat's Hole:* one of most famous bone-caves in Britain. Featureless at present owing to thorough excavations and not impressive in size, but with a fascinating pre-history and, archaeologically, has been 'the richest of British caves'. In 1823 headless human skeleton found by Dean Buckland, who named it 'The Red Lady of Paviland' because he took it to be female, of not very early date, and because it was dyed with red ochre. In 1913, excavation by Prof. Sollas established that it was of Paleolithic date. The skeleton was in

fact male and is now dated by radiocarbon to c.22,000 B.C. The red staining might result from burial rites, as a symbol of immortality. Remains of over 800 implements also found, together with bones of animals well suited to Ice Age climate. Interesting remains and a replica in SwM. but original 'Red Lady' is in University Museum, Oxford.

The cave is difficult to find and even more difficult of access, unless correct path and tide conditions are chosen. FP from main road (Finger post at edge of **Pilton Green**) ends at entrance to narrow craggy valley divided by stone wall. This can also be reached by cliffwalk from **Port-Eynon** (2m) or **Mewslade** (1½m). Follow FP down east side of valley to rocky inlet. Cave is on opposite side of gully, facing sea, but because of difficulty in crossing gully, access is really only practicable on about 8 days in the month, i.e. 2 days each side of spring (very low) tides. The cave is visible from the flat rocks, about 30 feet above sea level. The right hand (west) side of the valley is steep and dangerous and several people have been killed here.

2. *Paviland Western Cave:* 150 ft. W. of Goat's Hole and about same level above sea. Of no great interest. Fauna found possibly of Pleistocene origin.
4378578

Yellow Top is the limestone mass in which *Paviland Cave* is situated. An Iron Age promontory fort stands on top of this headland, defended on 3 sides by near vertical 150ft. cliffs. On the landward side four lines of banks and ditches protected the small settlement which existed here 2,000 years ago. So called because of the yellow orange lichens on the rock face, which are more conspicuous here than on most parts of the Coast.

PENCLAWDD (Welsh: 'end/head of the ditch/earthwork'). A large village of north-east ('Welsh') Gower (pop. 2,042). The name probably refers to the ancient hillfort of **Pen-y-gaer** on the hill above the village. Penclawdd began to develop in the 17th century and, by 1800, it was a thriving seaport with many coal mines and copper works. It revived briefly after a slump in the late 1800s, but most activity had stopped by 1900. The cockle industry, for which it was famed, is now centered on **Crofty** and **Llanmorlais**. The first of the Vivian family of industrialists, John Vivian, came from Cornwall and opened a works here in 1800 before moving on to lease land from the Duke of Beaufort at Hafod in the Lower Swansea Valley. There he founded a much larger enterprise. Copper bracelets manufactured in Penclawdd were used as currency in the West African slave trade. A railway served Penclawdd industry from 1866 to 1957, with a passenger service between 1867 and 1931. The village has a fine church, St. Gwynour at Llan-yr-newydd; it also has three large chapels: Tabernacle Presbyterian, Trinity Baptist, and Bethel Welsh Independent. The abandoned *Mount Hermon Chapel.* stands on a hillside south of the village overlooking the estuary.
See also Crofty
545959

PENGWERN COMMON (SSSI) Undulating open land, flanking the B4271 road 3m E. of **Llanrhidian**. With **Fairwood** and **Welshmoor** forms the landsker between English and Welsh Gower.
540920

PENMAEN (Welsh: stone head, end or top). Scattered village (pop. 165) along A4118 1m W. of *Parkmill*. Dominated by a building, the former workhouse, which later became an Old People's Home, originally 'Glan y môr' and then 'Three Cliffs Nursing Home'. Car parks.

The Church of St. John the Baptist has an obscure history, but it seems certain that it stood on its present site in the 14th century). An earlier church in the burrows occupied a site overlooking *Three Cliff Bay*. When this site was excavated during the last century, the evidence found suggested that it had been abandoned in the early 14th century; some of the objects discovered during this excavation are preserved in the SwM.

Lane (from main road) to *Tor Bay* and *Penmaen Burrows*. Talbot's Way (see *Cefn Bryn*) can be followed from behind the Three Cliffs Nursing Home building. The Gower Way can also be followed onto *Cefn Bryn* passing the *Gower Way Stone*.   **532887**

PENMAEN BURROWS An area of blown sand, coarse grass and bracken above the 200ft. limestone cliffs W. of *Three Cliff Bay*. The prominent rock off shore from here is known as *Benrick*. The name also occures in *Southgate* as *'Bendrick Drive'*. Four sites of archaeological interest are to be found on the burrows in close proximity to one another. They are:

1. *Penmaen Old Castle*. On the cliff edge overlooking Three Cliff Bay – a Norman defensive earth work of the 12th century. It consists of a massive stone bank fronted by a deep ditch. Excavation here in 1960 revealed remains of stone and timber buildings, and recovered the plan of the timber entrance tower, which had been burnt down in a fierce fire.   **535880**

2. *Penmaen Megalithic Tomb* (also referred to as *Pen-y-Crug*) 250 yds ENE. of above site. A good example of a large communal tomb of the first farming communities to arrive in Gower. Probably 5,500 years old. Note remains of entrance passage, and one remaining side chamber.   **532881**

3. *Old Church*. This is near the track leading to Old Castle, and is within 150 yards of the point where the lane from the main road opens on to the dunes. The first Penmaen Church stood here, and now consists only of a stone walled depression in the dunes. The Nave and Chancel can still be made out. It has been said that a whole village lies buried beneath the sand here.   **533882**

4. *Pillow Mound*. This large artificial rabbit warren is a fairly recent discovery and is not recorded on older OS maps. Warrens such as this have been constructed since Norman times when rabbits were first introduced as a source of meat and fur. This particular warren might have been associated with Penmaen Old Castle or could have been constructed for the Lord of the Manor in medieval times.   **534879**

40

Pennard Castle from the Pill

PENNARD A church without a village. The name is generally used to describe the housing developments at **Southgate** with its bus terminus and NT car park – also the whole of the adjacent cliffs.

The Church of St. Mary is surrounded by mystery, as there is a ruined church near Pennard castle on the sand dunes. The present building seems to have come into its own when castle and church were besanded in the early 16th century.

Lane due S. of church leads via **Widegate** to **Bishopston Valley**.

Pennard Cliffs. NT property consisting of a two mile stretch of open cliff-land from **Pwlldu Head** to **Three Cliff Bay**. Readily accessible from **Southgate** bus terminus and NT Car park. Several fine bone caves in this area, one of which is *Ravenscliff*; remains of mammoth, hippopotamus and lion have been found here. **565887**

The ruin of *Pennard Castle* which was probably built in the late 13th century and later be-sanded, occupies a commanding position overlooking the valley of the *Pennard Pill*.

See also Minchin Hole, Bacon Hole, Foxhole Bay, Hunts Bay, Forester's Cave, Pobbles Bay

Pennard Castle

PENNYHITCH *see Millwood*

PENRICE Small secluded village (pop. 46) between Penrice Park and the sea at **Oxwich**. Scarcely changed since the 18th cent. Once the social centre of Gower, on market and fair days, with prize-fighting, stepping and rowdy high jinks. The charter to hold a fair is still valid. Accessible only by steep and narrow roads, with few passing places. Nearby was the pound and the former village well is at the edge of **Millwood**. A large overgrown earthwork, the *Mountybank* marks the site of the first Norman fortress of Penrice.

41

Church of St. Andrew, Penrice

The Church of St. Andrew has retained much of its ancient character. In the churchyard, near to the porch, is a gravestone with an unusual inscription, the so-called 'Murder Stone'.

The base of the village cross is still on the green but the cross itself disappeared during the 18th century. **493879**

See also Margam Farm

PENRICE CASTLE 1. Norman castle in Penrice Park. **497885**
2. The modern 'castle', the only large country house of any age in Gower still used as a private residence. Built in the 18th century for Thomas Mansel Talbot, it is now occupied by the Methuen Campbell family. The building is on 4 floors, and has typical Georgian features, most notable being the massive, apse-like stone bay window on the south side. A large Victorian wing was added on the east side of the main block but has been demolished. A waymarked public footpath runs past the house between **Millwood** and the A4118. Close to this path, near the house, stands a small grove of trees planted over the years by Royal visitors to **Penrice**. In 1998 a tree was planted by HRH the Prince of Wales. **497884**

PEN-Y-CRUG An earthen Bronze Age barrow north of **Cefn Bryn** and near **Broad Pool**. About 2 miles west are four standing stones of unknown purpose, but which have been associated with boundary posts or even ley lines. **511913**

See also Penmaen Burrows

PERRISWOOD Farm and hamlet N. of A4118; ¼m N. of **Penrice Towers**. Some of the houses were originally built for Penrice Estate workers. FP to **Cefn Bryn** and **Penmaen**. **503887**

PILTON GREEN (uphill farm). Scattered settlement 2m E. of **Rhossili** where A4118 road opens out on to a small common (Pilton Green NT). Farms of East Pilton and West Pilton lie nearer Rhossili, between main road and cliffs.

Limited car parking space.

FP to **Paviland Caves**, and to **Old Henllys** passing ruin of Newton Farm. **437872**

PITT Large, impressive farmhouse (listed Grade II) on lane between *Penrice* and *Oxwich*. Built in early 17th cent., with drip stones over windows and corbelled chimney. Once home of Bennetts, a Gower family of some substance. References to Pitt as a landholding go back at least to 1516.

493871

PITTON (Farm in a hollow?). Sheltered settlement 1m E. of *Rhossili*, centred round Great Pitton Farm, one of oldest of Gower farms, has associations both with smuggling and with John Wesley. The Old Chapel Lane from A4118 road at foot of Pitton Hill (bus stop) leads down to *Mewslade* and Great Pitton, another in opposite direction leads up a little, wooded valley to Higher Pitton and FP across *Rhossili Downs* to *Llangennith* (3m N.).

428877

PITTON CROSS Two farms on small common (NT) at top of Pitton Hill 1m E. of *Pitton*. No cross roads so probably site of an ancient cross.

433878

Keenmore Lane is an old trackway leading from Pitton Cross to the back of *Rhossili Down*.

FP and bridleway, via Keenmore Lane, to Rhossili Down.

Three Cliff, from Pobbles

POBBLES BAY Popular but secluded sandy bay to east of *Three Cliff Bay*. Access from *Southgate* both on foot, following FP at side of golf links (1m), or along cliffs from Southgate NT carpark and bus terminus (1m).

540877

PORT-EYNON The name is thought to be derived from Eynon, who was one of the Welsh Princes in the 11th century and who was supposed to have built Port-Eynon Castle, long since disappeared. Paint material obtained

43

from a nearby 'mine' was, according to the Penrice Estate accounts of the 1870s, the origin of the GWR livery of chocolate brown and dull ochre!

Lifeboatman Memorial at Port-Eynon

The present village (pop. 247) surrounding the Church, with the houses on the side of narrow lanes extending to the beach. The Italian marble monument on side of main road near St. Cattwg Church is a memorial to members of the village lifeboat crew drowned during rescue duties in 1916. This caused the lifeboat to be withdrawn, as it was considered too hazardous an area. The old lifeboathouse at **Salthouse Quay** is now a Youth Hostel. The area around Salthouse and the Port-Eynon YH is *Crowders Quay*. At times in the summer, the lanes are busy, with the majority of cars heading to the Council-run car park near seashore on W. of village, or to the holiday chalets and caravan park on hill towards Horton. There is no direct road from the village itself to **Horton**, although it is linked by a bridleway. Likewise, **Overton** is either reached by FP or a turning off A 4118, on right just before Port-Eynon.

CP, shops, cafes, PH, YH, guesthouses, caravan and camping sites.
FPs along coast to Horton (½m) and inland to Overton (½m).   **468853**

PORT-EYNON BAY A fine curving mile of sands fringed with dunes (Burrows). Like all impressive sands on this coast, it lies to the lee of a prominent headland, here Port-Eynon Point. In the shelter of this Point the past seafaring life of the village evolved; in front of Crowders Quay cottages, traces of the oyster pools and old quays can still be seen. At one time forty oyster skiffs fished from here. Another activity in the 19th century being that limestone was quarried nearby and shipped across the Bristol Channel. The blue-green stones on the shore are not local, they were brought over as ballast by limestone ships from Devon. Smuggling, too, was a profitable occupation up to the end of the 18th century; there were at one time eight excise men stationed at Port-Eynon.

PORT-EYNON POINT (NT) is a good place from which to get a panoramic view of the whole of the Bay, with **Horton** to the E., stretching on to **Oxwich** Point. To the W. are the cliffs towards **Rhossili**. The standing stone at the top of the headland is a memorial to Dr. Gwent Jones and Mr. Stephen Lee: founder members of the Gower Society.

Off Port-Eynon Point, to the west, lies the *Helwick Sands* or *Helwick Bank*, a dangerous sandbank which is 7 miles long and which has been the site of many shipwrecks. The name is derived from the Norse, meaning a covered or hidden town, and horseshoes have been dredged up here by the oyster fishermen in the past. Local tradition tells of a castle where a buoy now marks the eastern limit of the Helwick Sands. A Lightship, which formerly marked the western end, is now outside the Swansea Industrial and

Maritime Museum, having been replaced by a radio buoy. Proposals in 1996 to double the amount of sand taken off the bank by commercial dredging have been the subject of much discussion, as the way by which sand moves between the Gower beaches and Helwick Sands is not yet fully understood. It is feared that increased dredging may result in a reduction of sand on these beaches

Port-Eynon Point Cave is at the tip of the Point: a bone-cave about 20ft. above sea level and inaccessible at HW. Track along shore westward around *Salthouse Mere* leads to cave. Animal remains in SwM and Nat.Hist.M (S. Kensington). **468844**

See also Salthouse, Culver Hole, Longhole, and Sedgers Bank

POUNDFFALD (*Ffald* is Welsh for 'pound', so on translation: 'Pound-pound'; a mixture of languages due to its being on border of old Welsh and English-speaking Gower.) A public house, which serves meals, bears the same name as the village; the remains of an ancient cattle pound are incorporated into the building. In addition, the site of a tollgate on the old turnpike road up from ***Penclawdd***; the area was the scene of 'Rebecca' riots in the early 19th century. **566945**

PRIOR'S TOWN Eastern end of ***Llangennith*** village, nearest the church. **430915**

PRISSEN'S TOR (*also known as Spritsail Tor*). Distinctive limestone headland at E. end of ***Broughton Bay***. In the north face of the Tor are a pair of accessible small caves linked by a low passage; these were discovered by two quarrymen in 1839. Animal remains, found in the caves in 1849, suggest that many thousands of years ago they served as hyenas' dens. **425937**

PWLLDU (Welsh = Blackpool) Where ***Bishopston Valley*** meets the sea. A vast storm beach of limestone pebbles dams the ***Bishopston*** stream. Sands at low water. No access by car. The parallel bands and ditches which run down the steep slopes of the headland on the W. of the bay and the pebbles of the storm beach are the relics of extensive limestone quarrying in the 19th century. This was once a large community, working the quarry. The two former public houses are now private residences and the ruins of many cottages can be found in the surrounding woodland. **575871**

Access on foot from ***Pyle Corner*** (1m E.) or ***Hunts Bay*** (2m W.). Footpath, up steps, to ***High Pennard***.

PWLLDU HEAD Twin headland forming the S.W. side of the bay at ***Pwlldu***, largely NT owned. Remains of an Iron Age promontory fort on west side. On east side, nearest to Pwlldu, is ***Bantam Bay***, the 'Ring Rock', and other reminders of the export trade in limestone. On south is ***Graves End*** and *Caesar's Hole*. **560862**

PYLE CORNER Between *Bishopston* and *Murton* where roads and footpaths lead off seawards to *Brandy Cove* and *Pwlldu*. These roads are very narrow and not recommended for cars because there is no parking or turning space at the end. There is a small group of shops near the main road. *See also Bishopston Valley, Hareslade* **580883**

PYLEWELL Group of houses on a rise in main road around old well 2m E. of *Rhossili*. This is the E. end of *Pilton Green*. Immanuel, one of Lady Barham's chapels, which she had built in 1821, is now a private hotel. *See Burry Green* **447870**

RAMSGROVE *see Thurba Head*

RATTLE STREET *see Llanmadoc*

RAVENSCLIFF *see Pennard*

RED CHAMBER Sea cavern ¼m E. of *Thurba Head*. Of no interest archaeologically; walls of cave colourful with red ochre, once extracted for commercial uses. At rear of cave, narrow tunnel made in search for lead in 19th cent. Shaft at end, now filled with water. Can be reached from cliff path from *Mewslade*. Not accessible at HW. **426866**

REYNOLDSTON (pop. 350). The name of the village is said to derive from Reginald de Breos, an early Lord of Gower, and its growth was due to reliable springs and wells providing good drinking water. Reynoldston is one of Gower's important settlements. Almost at the centre of the peninsula, it straggles along the western slopes of *Cefn Bryn*, a shapeless but pleasing village of greens and geese, bracken, stone walls, little streams from the hill, and fine long views, and housing the local office of the NT. This is a major meeting place of ways from N. and S.

King Arthur Hotel

PO, PH, shops.

Brynfield (*or Brynefield*) on the edge of the village, is one of the old houses of Gower and is listed G II. There seems to have been a substantial house here during the late medieval period. In Tudor times part of the Lucas family estate at Southall; during the mid-Victorian period it was the home of Sir Gardner Wilkinson, a distinguished Egyptologist and his wife, Caroline, who was a Lucas.

The original public house overlooking the Higher Green, (the village having two greens), was the Rising Sun; the remains of this building may be seen near the present King Arthur Hotel.

St. George's Church has beauty and dignity; one of the two bells in the gable is dated 1783, the other is unmarked. A Methodist Society was established in 1797, with the chapel built in 1877.

See Arthur's Stone, Cefn Bryn, Stouthall, Eynonsford, Fairyhill **480900**

RHOSSILI (pop. 253). Almost as many theories of where the name Rhossili originated as there are different spellings of the place name. One theory is that the name derives from the Welsh 'rhos', a moor and 'heti' meaning saltwater; hence 'moor by the sea'. An alternative theory is that the name comes from the name of the Lley stream coming off *Rhossili Down;* or lastly, from Fiji, a Celtic saint of St. Cenydd's college. However, a leading authority on Welsh place names has said that 'rhos' can also mean 'high land pushing into the sea' and that that is its meaning here, associated with the name 'Sulien'.

Rhossili is usually bracketed with *Middleton, Pitton and Pilton;* the area forms a unique corner of Gower. In a relatively small place, there is much to attract those interested in history, prehistory, flowers, rocks, seashore life, farming etc.; in fact, virtually everything covered in the various articles in this book. The only exception is 'trees'. A number of scrubby blackthorn and hawthorn bushes in the hedgerows, all sloping inland shaped by the gusty S.W. prevailing wind, is the Rhossili equivalent.

Even as late as 1900, Rhossili had changed little from previous centuries, when the main road ended at Pitton Cross. These days, the B4247 ends in the village, as does the bus service from Swansea. The houses are scattered around St. Mary's Church perched on top of the 200 foot cliffs, at the most western part of Gower. *The Viel* is the ancient strip field system of Rhossili, extending from the Church to the headland. It is a system of sharing out the best land in the parish. A large proportion of the land has been bought by the NT to safeguard the system. The relatively frost-free conditions suit the growing of early crops, including potatoes. The dramatic cliffs, headland and foreshore, including *Worms Head*, belong to the NT; the area draws over a third of a million visitors every year. There is a NT Visitor Centre and shop in the former coastguard cottages. The village has cafes, telephone, toilets, CP (privately owned), hotel with bar, guest-houses and coastguard.

Walks radiate out of Rhossili in most directions: the FP to *Fall Bay* starts opp. Church and passes through the *Viel.* There are paths to the splendid beach and also up *Rhossili Down* (passing old Rocket House, where up until 60 years ago, rocket equipment for 'bosun's chair' rescues was kept). One popular cliff walk is on the surfaced track alongside the drystone wall to terminate at one end of *The Gower Way* near the CCW information centre in a former coastguard lookout. Starting near the toilets, it passes the former coastguard cottages and the 'Old Castle', and Iron Age camp. As on all Gower cliff walks, particular care is needed if walking near cliff edge.   **417881**

RHOSSILI BAY The unspoiled beach is claimed to be one of the best in Britain. The Bay is framed by the tidal islands of *Worms Head* at the southern tip and *Burry Holms* on the northern end; both islands are well worth a visit when the tidal conditions allow. It must be noted that the crossing to Worms Head can mean walking on rocky and slippery surfaces. Fatalities have occurred here and advice from the coastguard should be obtained before attempting a crossing at any time. The complete arc of the

Bay is five miles; the beach itself being three miles long. When the wind is high, the unbroken sand is often scoured by Atlantic rollers; so whether on a good day or a bad one, the view is spectacular and it is a popular surfing beach.

Tales of smuggling and shipwrecks form a link with the past: the wooden ribs of the *Helvetia*, driven ashore in 1887, can still be seen at the **Rhossili** end of the Bay. At the opposite end, during low water, part of the iron hulk of *The City of Bristol*, a small paddle-steamer homeward bound from Waterford, which ran ashore in 1840 is visible. In the second half of the 17th century, the 'dollar ship' reputed to have been carrying the dowry of a Portuguese princess (?Catherine of Braganza, who became the Queen of Charles II), was wrecked. In 1807 and 1833, quantities of silver coins were uncovered by the tides and found by villagers. Some of the coins, identified as Peruvian dollars of Phillip IV, still exist in SwM and Nat.MW.

At the raised terrace along side the S. end of the Bay is an area of sand dunes called the Warren, owned by the NT; during excavations in 1979 archaeologists discovered the remains of a 'lost village'. Parts of a church and some houses were discovered; it is claimed that these could date back to pre-Norman times. The settlement is considered to have been abandoned in the early 14th century, most likely due to economic decline and gradual encroachment of the sand.

The isolated house near the centre of the raised terrace above the bay was an old parsonage, Rhossili Rectory; it was built when the living at Rhossili was combined with that at **Llangennith**. The present house, rebuilt in the 1850s, stands on a site which is thought to have associations with the Knights of St. John. The Old Rectory was renovated in 1996, and is now a NT holiday house.

RHOSSILI DOWN At 193m (632ft.). *The Beacon* is the highest point in Gower; the climb is rewarded by 360 degree views of the peninsula, the Bristol Channel and Carmarthen Bay. Paths to the top start at **Rhossili** and also an easier climb from **Middleton**. As at **Cefn Bryn**, scattered stones, cairns and round barrows indicate the use of these hill tops as burial grounds over thousands of years. The oldest of all are **Sweyne's Howes**. A much more recent ruin, the former World War II prototype radar station, is situated in a hollow on the W. slopes of the Downs.

See Burry Holms, Fall Bay, Kitchen Corner, Mewslade Bay, Paviland Caves, Pitton, Thurba

ROTHERSLADE *see Langland Bay*

RYER'S DOWN Sandstone hill 114m. high between **Burry Green** and **Cheriton**. Some NT land. Extensive views.   **458921**

SALTHOUSE The strange and forlorn ruins, reached by footpath which mark the western end of **Port-Eynon Bay** are the gable ends of a pair of cottages erected here in the 18th century, and occupied until the middle of the 19th century. The sea washes to the edge of the ruins, and at low water the remains of more massive structures, including heavy stone vaulting, can be seen on the nearby beach.

These are all that the sea has left of a stone quay and salt pans which may have been part of the notable mansion of Salthouse, once a principal seat of the Lucas family.

The mansion remained in the hands of seven generations of the Lucas family, until it was severely damaged in a violent storm, probably the notorious Great Storm of 1703. The Lucas' had become rich by a variety of means: sale of salt was one, another was the exploitation of paint material found on the land, others were reputed to be rather less legal!

Two simple cottages were built on the site and they, in their turn, have fallen into ruin.

Conservation work has been carried out on the ruins and the salt pans; explanation boards are in place. **468847**

Salthouse Mere is a small inlet under **Port-Eynon Point** separated from the Bay by a ridge of rock leading to **Sedgers Bank**.

See also Culver Hole

SALTHOUSE POINT 1½m E. of **Penclawdd** at Crofty near where the Morlais River turns into Salthouse Pill, thence into the estuary mud. **520956**
See Crofty

SAMSON'S JACK Standing stone W. of **Oldwalls** in field S. of Windmill Farm. **477923**

SANDS (THE) sandy inlet also known as '*Slade Bay*' in the rocky coast E. of **Horton** reached by coastal FP from Horton or around point from **Oxwich**. **487854**

SANCTUARY Listed Grade II Farmhouse near **Penrice** on lane leading to **Horton**. Once property of Knights of St. John. Said to incorporate 14th century masonry. **488875**

SANDY LANE (i) Lane across the dunes linking **Parkmill** (opp. Guide Centre) to **Southgate** (opposite Pennard School)
(ii) Chalet settlement situated off Sandy Lane. **548888**

SCURLAGE. A post World War II motel and small housing estate on B4247 at junction of **Rhossili** and **Porteynon** roads. Sports field, chalets. During World War II the site was an American Army camp, due to the nearby beaches of **Oxwich, Port-Eynon** and **Rhossili** resembling the beaches of Normandy; the lane down to Oxwich, off the A4118, is still known as the American Road. After D-Day the camp was used to house Italian prisoners of war. PH, shop.

A ¼m nearer Swansea, was a manor house, Scurlage Castle, built in 14th century by Sir Herbert Scurlage who married into the Mansel family; now in private ownership. **463882**

SEDGERS BANK and **SKYSEA** Two protective ridges of sand and rocks below *Port-Eynon Point*; accessible only along the shore. Both ridges become islands at spring tides and in stormy weather. The last member of the Lucas family to live at the *Salthouse*, the ruined house situated nearby on the coast, is reputed to be buried on Sedgers Bank. Skysea is a popular crabbing area. **473844**

SLADE Hamlet W. of *Oxwich Green* which also includes the two farms of Western Slade and Eastern Slade.
FPs from *Horton* (lm) and down the valley from eastern end of *Oxwich Green*. **486855**
See Sands, The

SLUXTON Remote, typical Welsh Longhouse farm dating from 18th century. Near path to *Llangennith* across *Rhossili Downs* (1½m N. of *Middleton*). Name thought to derive from Sir Hortonk Van Klux who took over Llangennith Priory between 1431 and 1435. **428897**

SMUGGLERS' LANE *see Highway*

SOUTHEND *see Oystermouth*

SOUTHGATE (pop. 1,758). Once a small hamlet, now much enlarged, near Pennard Golf Club, the oldest golf club on Gower. PO, cafe, shops, toilets, NT car park and leaflets. Terminus for Swansea buses. Often referred to as *'Pennard'*. **550880**
FPs on Cliffs (NT) to *Three Cliff Bay* (1½m W.) and *Hunts Bay* (1m E.).
See Foxhole

SPRITSAIL TOR *see Prissen's Tor*

ST. PETER'S WELL *see Caswell Valley* **594883**

STAVEL-HAGAR Former woollen factory (listed Grade IV), along inland edge of marshes, ½m W. of *Llanrhidian*. The weaving family here were the Dixes; looms dismantled in 1904. Now 'Gower Water' is bottled on this site. **496824**

STEMBRIDGE A large two-arched stone bridge carries the road from *Llanrhidian* to *Llangennith* over the Burry Stream. Nearby is site of former Stembridge Mill, a 19th century woollen factory and one of the many mills along the Burry stream
FPs to *Cheriton* across *Ryer's Down* and along valley. **468917**

STONEMILL *see Parkmill*

STOUTHALL (Formerly Stout Walls). Imposing country house (built *c.*1800) in once elegant park, near junction of A4118 at *Knelston* with lane to *Reynoldston*. Was the home of the Lucas family, who spread throughout

Gower. Subsequently, was used as a maternity home and then a study centre for the London Borough of Merton.

In a field opposite (E.) was a pre-Norman pillar stone, found by a Lucas and erected here in early 19th cent., some say over the grave of his horse. The Stone is now in *Reynoldston* Church. The stone circle, a Lucas folly, which once stood in a field to W. of lane (¼m to N.E. of Stouthall), was removed in 1998.   **475893**

SWANSEA AIRPORT After passing through *Upper Killay*, Swansea Airport is the main feature to be seen on *Fairwood Common*. The Airport was constructed during the Second World War as a R.A.F. fighter station. Unfortunately, two Bronze Age barrows or 'burchs' had to be destroyed during its contruction. Cinerary urn from one of the sites, 'Bishopston burche' is in SwM. Now used mainly for private and pleasure flights, flying school and aircraft museum. There is a cafe which is open to the public.   **570913**

SWEYNE'S HOWES (*or Swine Houses or Sweyn's Houses*). Situated on E. slopes of *Rhossili Down* are two megalithic tombs. Tradition has it that this is the burial place of Sweyn, the Scandinavian sea-lord who may have given his name to Swansea (Sweyn's-ey).   **422898**

TALBOT'S WAY *see Cefn Bryn*

TALGARTH'S WELL An ancient well and cottage near *Middleton*. The water was highly prized for buttermaking due to its coldness.   **428881**

TANKEYLAKE MOOR Level open moor between *Llangennith* road and *Llanmadoc Hill*. There is a story that the occupants of the Bulwark Hill Fort met those of the *Hardings Down* Fort here and were defeated in a battle. Their leader, one Tonkin, was killed and the blood rose above the warriors' boots – hence TANKEYLAKE.   **434915**

TEARS POINT (NT) Headland to W. of *Fall Bay*.   **410870**

THE BEACON *see Rhossili*   **420888**

THREE CLIFF BAY (*popularly known as Three Cliffs Bay*). One of the most photographed places in Gower. Wide sandy estuary of the *Pennard* pill. Sand dunes and salt marsh to the W., the three pointed cliffs which name the bay to the east. Bathing should not be attempted – very dangerous currents. Footpath from *Parkmill* (1m), and over stepping stones by old track up to *Penmaen* (1m). Can be reached also by FP along cliffs from Southgate (1½m).   **536877**

See Pennard

Archway, Three Cliff Bay

THREE CROSSES ('Y Crwys'), (pop. 1,178). A large and straggling north Gower village, with a number of modern housing developments. Formerly scattered mining cottages with some old farms such as Crwys, Killan, etc. The village is dominated by the large 'Capel y Crwys' (1877) designed by John Humphrey, of Morriston Tabernacle fame. The Welsh Independent chapel is associated also with the Prices of Cwrt y Carne, on the *Loughor* estuary. **569943**

THURBA (HEAD) (NT) Impressive 200ft. headland forming E. side of *Mewslade* Bay. Iron Age promontory fort. Accessible by lane from Great Pitton Farm, or by sheep track up from Mewslade Bay. No cars. Nearest parking: *Pitton* (very limited but field open for parking with honesty box). A small rocky inlet on E. side of *Thurba Head* is known as *Butterslade*. *Ramsgrove*, is a rocky pebble inlet W. of *Paviland* and ½m E. of *Thurba Head*. Winding inland, a fine slade, typical of Gower – broad, wild and craggy, with scree piled at foot of high bare cliffs – of glacial origin. **421868**

TOR BAY At eastern end of *Oxwich Bay*. Popular sandy bay with steep approaches and with the dramatic pinnacle of the *Great Tor* on its eastern side. Accessible by footpaths from *Penmaen* (1m). A large restored limekiln, one of many remnants of the once important lime industry in Gower, stands at the head of the bay. Other restored limekilns can be seen near *Kilvrough Manor*, in *Green Cwm*, and at *Landimore*. Lime burning was a significant industry in Gower between 1800 and 1960 but was past its peak by 1913. Small quarries and ruined kilns are still dotted around Gower; most were run by individual farmers to supply agricultural lime to their own and nearby farms. A commercial kiln operated at Hills near *Llanmadoc* until the 1930s and the kilns at Colts Hill, *Oystermouth*, were filled in during the early 1960s. Here the Norton Lime Works switched to making asphalt before eventually closing down in the 1970s. **528877**
See also Old Henllys

TOWERS, THE On main S. road (A4118). Western gateway to Penrice Park, at junction with road down to *Oxwich*. The picturesque ruins of curtain wall of castle and drum tower are imitation, a 19th cent. folly of the Talbot family, which was once used as a lodge and occupied by estate staff. **502884**

TRINITY WELL *see Ilston Cwm*

TRUMPET LANE *see Knelston*

TUTT HEAD Small headland between *Limeslade Bay* and *Bracelet Bay*, now site of Coastguard Control Centre. **628871**

TWLC POINT Small, low, limestone headland on west of *Broughton Bay*. Separates the wide expanse of Broughton Bay from the more intimate Little Broughton. **416932**

UPPER KILLAY Continues on from *Killay* (B4271), although originally part of *Bishopston* parish; here suburbia gives way to the open expanse of *Fairwood Common*. Cattle grids on road are to prevent sheep, cattle and ponies straying off the common. Take care, as on all Gower roads, to avoid the animals. Petrol, shop, TIC. **585927**

VENNAWAY LANE *see Kilvrough Manor*

VIEL, THE (pron. vile) *see Rhossili*

WALTERSTON Farm off northern slopes of *Cefn Bryn* 1m N.E. of *Penmaen*. Once, with *Cillibion*, belonged to Neath Abbey. The remnants of the strip field system of the former hamlet of Walterston can still be discerned near the farm. **515895**

WELSH MOOR Open moorland 1m east of *Llanrhidian*. The name is a reminder that this was a boundary (*or landskeer*) in former times between 'Welsh Gower' (*Gower Wallicana*) and 'English Gower' (*Gower Anglicana*). **520930**

WEOBLEY CASTLE (CADW) 1m N.W. of *Oldwalls*, open to public (charge), access from road to *Cheriton*. Fine, dominating position and view over the marshes of the *Burry Estuary*. The tower at the end of the private concrete road out onto the marsh is the 'Spotting Tower' used during the 1939-45 war when the area was a firing range. **477927**

Weobley Castle

WERNBWLL Above *Blue Anchor* where a large colliery was operated from *Berthllwyd* between 1893 and 1931. On 28th November 1929 seven men were killed in a gas explosion and the mine never really recovered. The site of the mine is marked with a memorial to the men killed and the area has been landscaped to include footpaths and a picnic spot with parking. **554947**

WERNFFRWD (Welsh: 'Gwernffrwd' – alder stream). A hamlet near the Marsh Road between *Llanmorlais* and *Llanrhidian* at the edge of the Burry marshes with medieval origins as a farming settlement. Important for mining from about 1620 up to 1900. Also connected with the cockle industry. Nearby is the building which was formerly St. David's Mission Room. **517941**

WERN-HALOG (Welsh: 'gwern = alder and 'halog' = muddy). Formerly a farm of medieval origin between *Crofty* and *Llanrhidian*. **507932**

WERNLLATH Two farms, Upper and Lower, between *Clyne Common* and *Barland Common*. Formerly a hamlet of up to twelve houses and a pub. Wernllath was a division in the parish of Bishopston.   589905

WHITEFORD BURROWS AND SANDS Wild expanse of dune and pine plantation running north of *Llanmadoc* into the *Burry Estuary* (1¼m) to Whiteford Point, where there is an old lighthouse, the only sea washed cast iron lighthouse in UK; now being preserved. Flanked on west by fine, secluded, two-mile sweep of Whiteford Sands. National Nature Reserve and NT property. Walkers only. Keep to beach or footpath.   444945 – 447966
See also Berges Island

WHITE MOOR Former woollen factory on eastern slopes of *Rhossili Down*, 1m S. of *Llangennith*. Now a house. Wheel still remains and traces of mill pond can still be seen. On FP from *Coety Green* to *Rhossili*.
                                                                            427902

WIDEGATE (pron. Wijet). Once a cottage in *Bishopston Valley* with date stone 1771. Replaced by a modern house. On lane leading from Pennard Church towards *Pwlldu*.   566881

WORMS HEAD (O.E. wurm = dragon). Locally known as 'the Worm'. Mile long serpent-like promontory at most westerly tip of peninsula. The Shipway between the Inner Head and the mainland begins to be exposed to ebb tide, 2½ to 3 hours after HW. Between Middle and Outer Heads is bridge of rock *(Devil's Bridge)*. Along Outer Head, the Blow Hole, where air is forced through cleft in the rock-face by wave action on north face of Worm.
A Nature Reserve; fascinating in richness of flowers and sea-birds, which are protected and should be disturbed as little as possible. Nature Reserve visitors are requested to keep away from the outer parts between mid March and July, when birds are nesting.
Warning. Before going out check time of tides, and leave Worm for mainland *not later than 3½ hours* before next HW.   384877 – 405872

YELLOW TOP *see Paviland Caves*

ZOAR *see Crofty*
                                          ★

ORIGINAL GAZETTEER
compiled by J. Mansel Thomas.

1999 EDITION
based on the original,
but completely revised and updated by
Don Strawbridge and Peter Thomas.

54

THE CASTLES OF GOWER

The Normans took possession of Gower at the beginning of the twelfth century. They came into South Wales as relatively small bands of military adventurers, seizing on the disunity and weakness of the Welsh rulers to dispossess them and to establish their new lordships, of which Gower was one. Each new lordship was further sub-divided into individual manors, parcelled out among the chief lord's more important followers.

In many of the new manors, the invaders erected defences consisting of earth and stone mounds and banks, protected by ditches. These were the first castles built in Gower, and examples can still be seen at Penrice village (the 'Mounty Bank'), Barland Old Castle (Bishopston), and Penmaen Old Castle ('Castle Tower'). The earthworks at Norton Mount, near Oxwich, and at North Hill Tor, near Cheriton, are likely to be of this period also.

These simple castles were severely mauled on several occasions in Welsh counter attacks, but the Normans and their English followers resisted, until in the last half of the thirteenth century the building of the stone castles we see today marked the collapse of Welsh resistance. Some of the stone castles are described on the following pages and of these, Pennard and Oystermouth both stand on the sites of older, simpler castles, such as those described above. Weobley, which is also included, was a fortified manor house rather than a castle. Just one mile to the west of it are the remains of yet another large fortified manor house, known as Landimore Castle. Although in advanced decay, enough survives there to show that this included a very large hall with private rooms for the lord and extensive service rooms arranged around a defensible courtyard. It was probably built in the 1450s for Sir Hugh Johnys, lord of the manor of Landimore at that time.

Although these pages deal with the castles within the Gower peninsula, it should not be forgotten that the lordship of Gower extended far to the north and that Llwchwr Castle and Swansea Castle were held by its chief lord in his own hands. Swansea Castle once covered a much larger area than it does today and the fine arcaded parapet, added in about the 1340s, shows that what remains was a building of distinction and importance, the chief castle of the whole lordship of Gower.

OYSTERMOUTH

It is likely that a castle was established here soon after 1100, probably by the de Londres family, who also held Ogmore Castle. The oldest surviving masonry is in the southern half of the central block, which began as a rectangular hall or keep, very similar to that at Ogmore. Later the castle and manor of Oyster-mouth came into the direct ownership of the lords of Gower, who used it as an alternative to Swansea Castle as a residence, fortress and prison. With other castles in Gower, Oystermouth suffered in various Welsh attacks during the twelfth and thirteenth centuries, but was repaired and extended. Much of what remains today was the work of the de Breos family, and was prob-ably completed in time for the visit of Edward I in 1284, on his triumphal tour of Wales following the defeat of Llewellyn 'the last'. The gatehouse is unusual, and although its twin towers have been demolished (or may never have been built), the plan is very similar to the gatehouses at the royal castle at Rhuddlan. Within three years of his visit, the castle was taken during a forlorn but fierce Welsh rising. Whatever damage was caused, the castle was repaired and at some time around 1330 or so it was extended again, for the last time, by the building of the massive north-eastern tower. The top floor of this contained a fine private chapel, with traceried windows which are still prominent features. The castle remained in the hands of the chief lords of Gower, serving as a country seat, courthouse and prison for several cen-turies, but in 1650 it was described as 'an old decayed castle . . . being for the present of noe use, but of a very pleasant scituaton and near unto the sea side'.

PENNARD

The twin D-shaped gate towers and single arched gateway still mark the only entrance, and help to date the present castle to the period when the Norman conquests were consolidated in the later years of the thirteenth century. The northern curtain wall survives but the narrow rampart walk must once have been supplemented by a timber platform. Most of the southern curtain wall, exposed to the south-westerly winds, has fallen. On a sheer rock overlooking the valley is a projecting square building added against the outside of the curtain wall. The present stone curtain walls stand on the remains of a rubble bank which enclosed and defended this site in the troubled years of the twelfth century. Traces of this were found during excavations in 1961, which also recovered the plan of the hall of this early castle. The hall was built of well-mortared stone and it had the twin store-rooms, large com-munal living area and private retiring room typical of the period. The remains were reburied to preserve them but some traces can still be seen. The location is superb, but Pennard Castle is rarely mentioned in surviving records, and in 1650 it was 'desolate and ruinous'. The encroachment of the sand appears to have commenced soon after the stone castle was completed. Near the gatehouse are the scanty remains of what was probably once the parish church, replaced in the sixteenth century by the present church on a site over a mile away, well beyond the reach of the encroaching sand.

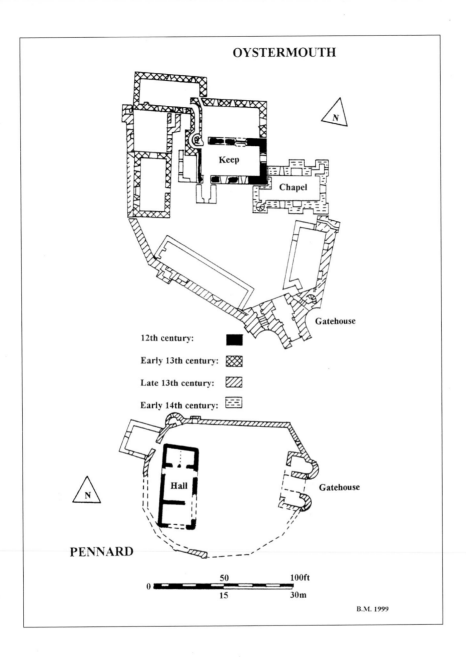

OYSTERMOUTH

N

Keep

Chapel

Gatehouse

12th century:

Early 13th century:

Late 13th century:

Early 14th century:

N

Hall

Gatehouse

PENNARD

0   50   100ft
    15   30m

B.M. 1999

WEOBLEY

Weobley Castle is well-fortified, but its crenellations and corbels are subordinate to its domestic arrangements. Its picture-book towers are slender and contain only stairways and latrines. The 'castle' is in fact a fortified manor house. Most of the surviving buildings were built in the early fourteenth century and are grouped around a courtyard. There is a simple gatehouse on the west, with private apartments for the lord of the castle between it and the spacious great hall on the north. Kitchens and service rooms stand on the east, and on the south is a room over which the castle chapel once stood. At the south-western corner is the base of a massive square tower, once, but not currently, thought to have been the oldest work on the site. Until the fifteenth century the castle belonged to the de la Bere family, and later illustrious owners included Sir Rhys ap Thomas, the Herbert family and the Mansels. In about 1403, during Owain Glyndŵr's rising, the buildings were extensively damaged, but were soon repaired and in use again. From the seventeenth century the castle served as a farmhouse. In 1911, it was placed in the care of the State and it is now maintained by Cadw.

PENRICE

Penrice is the largest castle in Gower, and its entrance is appropriately flanked by two massive towers, flat-sided, but with rounded corners. It stands on a steep sided promontory within the private grounds of Penrice Park. The gate towers and the tall curtain wall with its small rounded bastions were built in the last quarter of the thirteenth century, together with the long gable-ended building in the interior of the castle. The fine stone pigeon-house outside the south-western curtain was probably added a couple of centuries later. The gatehouse and curtain were erected to strengthen a simpler structure of which only the round keep, built about 1240, and some fragments of early curtain wall, remain. Adjoining the keep, which stands to the south-west of the gatehouse, is a complex group of buildings which formerly comprised the main hall and two projecting towers, all now very much ruined. This group was added soon after the completion of the gatehouse and curtain wall. The extensive building work strained the resources of the lords of Penrice without curtailing their influence. In the Wars of the Roses, Phillip Maunsell of Penrice was an active supporter of the Lancastrian cause. His grandson, Sir Rice Mansel of Penrice, Oxwich and Margam, attained high office under Henry VIII, and established the Mansels among the great landowners of South Wales.

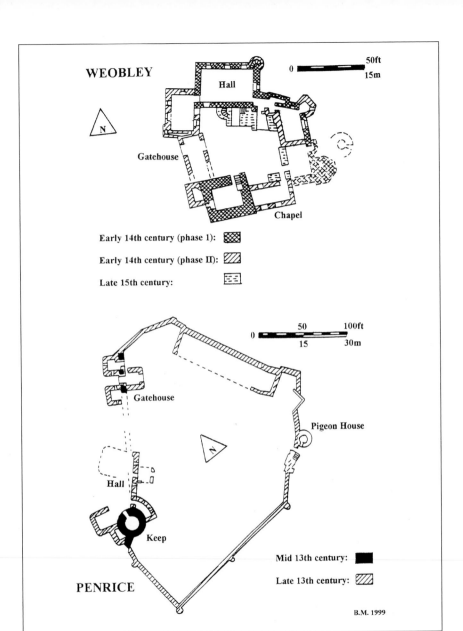

WEOBLEY

Hall

50ft
0 ▬▬▬▬▬ 15m

N

Gatehouse

Chapel

Early 14th century (phase 1): ▨

Early 14th century (phase II): ▨

Late 15th century: ▨

Gatehouse

Pigeon House

N

Hall

Keep

PENRICE

Mid 13th century: ■

Late 13th century: ▨

50   100ft
0 ▬▬▬▬▬
15   30m

B.M. 1999

OXWICH

Oxwich Castle stands high above the village amongst the trees overlooking Oxwich Bay. Although fragments of an earlier castle exist within its walls, most of the visible structure dates from the sixteenth century. The castle survived proposals for its demolition in 1949 and is now cared for by Cadw, the Welsh ancient monuments body, after many years of consolidation work. Its late date, vast areas of living accommodation and relatively weak defences show that the building could more accurately be described as a 'mansion' than as a 'castle'. Its buildings stand around a roughly square courtyard, entered through a simple but impressive gateway which bears an heraldic plaque with the arms and initials of Sir Rice Mansel (1487-1559).

Across the courtyard, opposite the gateway, stands a huge wall with many blocked windows and doorways in it. This is the western side of the hall block, once the centre of life in the castle, but its eastern side collapsed long ago. Although so much is missing, enough remains to show that the hall, at first floor level and rising through two complete floors, lay in the centre of this block. Below it was a stone-vaulted basement and above it was a range of large rooms, the window openings of which still indent the top of the wall. At its north end were service rooms, including the kitchen, and at the south end were the family's private apartments. There were broad stairs at each end, but only that at the family end reached to the top floor. The remains of all these features can still be seen.

On the south side of the courtyard is the much lower block which became a farmhouse when the castle was no longer needed by the Mansel family. It now houses the visitor centre and exhibitions. Although the collapse of part of the hall block at its junction with the farmhouse block has complicated interpretation, enough remains to show (despite some suggestions to the contrary) that the farmhouse block is the later of the two, having been built up against the already existing structure of the hall. It is likely that Sir Rice Mansel carried out most of the rebuilding work at the castle, including the hall. Later the family's principal seat moved to Beaupre (by 1526) and then to Margam, and the hall block at Oxwich would have become too large for that castle's reduced status. The addition of what later became the farmhouse block would then have provided more manageable and convenient accommodation.

The castle gateway was the scene of a violent incident in 1557, when during a dispute over goods recovered from a wreck, followers of Sir Rice Mansel clashed there with those of Sir George Herbert, steward of the lord of Gower. Anne Mansel, sister in law of Sir Rice, was mortally wounded by a stone thrown by one of Sir George's followers. This serious matter reached the Court of Star Chamber, and the legal records cast a detailed if lurid light on this dispute between two leading gentry families.

Bernard Morris

60

OXWICH

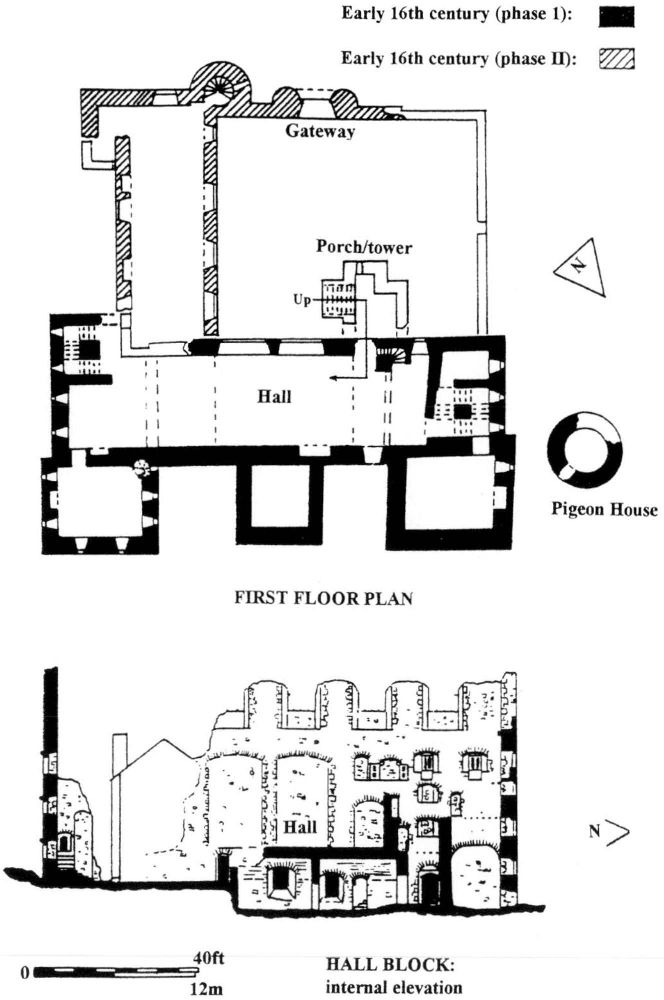

Early 16th century (phase 1): ■
Early 16th century (phase II): ▨

Gateway

Porch/tower

Up

Hall

N

Pigeon House

FIRST FLOOR PLAN

Hall

N

0 — 40ft / 12m

HALL BLOCK:
internal elevation

B.M. 1999

61

ANIMAL LIFE IN GOWER

In addition to coastal cliffs, sand dunes and salt marshes, Gower, although of relatively small area, contains a wide variety of woodlands, scrub country and open commons situated on both acid and limestone soils; this variety of habitats results in great richness of plant and animal life. Most species of British mammal have been observed at some time, including an abundance of the larger species such as the badger and the otter. All British reptile species occur, apart from the smooth snake and the continental lizards, although the sand lizard is now rare. The small streams, which are limited in size and number, and marshes contain many species of fish and amphibia, the palmate newt being a common species. In the past, many ponds in Gower, as in so many parts of Britain, dried up or were filled with rubbish. It is thus particularly fortunate that the Glamorgan Wildlife Trust was given Broad Pool (Cillibion), a two-acre body of water in a clay-lined depression which contains a wide variety of animal and plant life, including a range of dragonfly species, many water bugs and a very rich microscopic fauna. The Burry Pill contains many species of fish, including the sewin and brown trout, and the Parkmill stream includes the ammocoete larva of the Lamprey amongst other interesting species.

The invertebrate animals of Gower are equally diverse and it is difficult to select species for special mention. Specialists in particular groups will certainly have their own sources of information about good localities and those who are interested will doubtless contact the School of Biological Sciences of the University of Wales Swansea, where records are available. The acquisition of a number of sites as reserves has protected them from 'development'. The sand dunes, with their rich flora, are particularly notable for an outstanding variety of spiders and beetles, some species being known only from this area of Britain. But half an hour's observation on a sunny day will certainly impress even the novice with the range of species and the remarkable camouflage which allows many of them to blend with their background of sandy or grassy stems.

The cliffs and the salt marshes have species new to Britain and to science. Of many generally interesting features, there is space to mention only the remarkable salt marsh pools which are filled at spring tides with salt water, dried out between tides and almost as often flooded with rain water. Their fauna contains both freshwater and marine elements and these must possess remarkable adaptations to such a range of conditions. Secondly the limestone cliffs have a rich fauna of snails and insects whose distribution appears to reflect the strong contrasts in soil conditions which result from local flushing by alkaline water in a climate otherwise notable for leaching by heavy rainfall. The intertidal zone on limestone rocks, sandy and muddy shores displays interesting examples of insects approaching the marine environment.

The Gower woods and commons have been spared, until recently, the attentions of the farmer and the forester, and the Forestry Commission has shown great consideration for the interests of amenity. This results in a notable variety of woodland insects and other small creatures, amongst which the snails and beetles have provided records of outstanding interest. Rare species present include a rare strand-line beetle (*Eurynebria complanata*) and a spider named after Gower (*Lisiargus gowerensis*).

But it must be stressed that, although exhibiting an outstanding variety of habitats these are of limited extent and vulnerable. The Nature Conservancy Council (NCC) has three National Nature Reserves on Gower, and other bodies look after designated areas. Gower, therefore, has much to offer the student of animal life. Although pressures increase annually, great efforts are made to try and preserve this area in a relatively unspoiled condition. How long this situation will last will depend to a large extent on the willingness of our visitors to forego some of the amenities of a seaside resort area in favour of retaining unspoiled the wildlife of a small and very vulnerable region.

Phillip King

BIRDS IN GOWER

The cliffs and salt marshes, the tidal flats, shingle and sandy beaches, the pills meandering into wide estuaries, the high windswept moors, the wooded valleys, the farmed lands on which hedgerows weave an intricate pattern, all provide, in the narrow confines of the peninsula, a great variety of habitats attractive to a correspondingly large number of species. There are elsewhere more dramatic and impressive sites, but Gower earns the regard in which ornithologists hold it by offering well rewarded observation throughout the year in easy travelling distance.

To describe the birdlife comprehensively would be difficult without seeming to draw up a mere checklist, but experience has taught which groups of birds to expect at a given favoured site at any season of the year. So, early on, say in January or February, one goes with great benefit to Whiteford Point and Berges Island. Start at Cheriton and walk down Frog Lane. High above the left bank of the Burry Pill, rooks will be in evidence, some foraging in the fields, others flying high over the taller trees, above the lane, where later there will be a noisy nesting colony. With luck, you might see a pair of ravens performing aerobatics over North Hill Tor. Other resident members of the crow family in Gower are carrion crow, jackdaw, magpie, jay and, since the late 1980s, the chough, which has made a welcome return to breed on our cliffs after an absence of nearly a hundred years. The best place to observe these pugnacious red-billed, red-legged crows is from East Cliff at Pennard, though their distinctive calls may now be heard almost anywhere along the South Gower cliffs.

As you descend Frog Lane, there will be many small birds in the shrubs and low trees: great, blue, coal, marsh and long-tailed tits may all be found. The willow tit is listed in *Gower Birds* as a scarce breeding resident and may be looked for and found in nearby Cheriton Woods in spring. Soon the green woodpecker will be heard 'yaffling' and perhaps seen crossing the valley in undulating flight. The greater spotted woodpecker is also listed as a common breeding resident and may be heard drumming in Cheriton Woods.

The old quarry just this side of Pill House marks the border of a Trust Nature Reserve. Nuthatches, treecreepers and wrens haunt these tangled woods winter and summer, though of course, like all resident birds, they are subject to local movement according to wind, weather and food supply. The footpath to Whiteford now continues along an ancient seawall which pro-tects the pastures of Cwm Ivy against the high tides that can roll over the whole of the Groose. Here lapwing, curlew and redshank may be picking about in the withered grass and sedge, though not, alas, in former large numbers. You may also see flocks of fieldfare and redwing; both are regular winter visitors whose numbers increase with harder weather, with ever more and more reaching the relatively mild climate of West Wales from Scandinavia. They are members of the thrush family, otherwise represented in Gower by the familiar resident song and mistle thrushes, the blackbird and the scarce ring ouzel, the latter only occasionally spotted, perhaps once or twice a year, on its way to the hills.

At the west end of the seawall, the path turns northwest-by-north, skirt-ing the sand dunes of Whiteford Burrows on the left and, on the right, the Great Plain, a wide saltmarsh criss-crossed by numerous creeks deeply cut into the soft brown ooze. Here live skylarks and meadow pipits and when you reach the conifer plantation you will often find a mixed flock of finches and tits, which may include bramblings. A lesser spotted woodpecker may turn up. The maturing Corsican pines now attract crossbills, which even at this time of year may already be breeding high in the branches.

At Berges Island or from the beach near the old lighthouse huge mur-murations of starlings may be seen crossing the estuary, usually flying from the Pembrey side to Gower in the early morning and large flocks of oyster-catchers, disturbed from their feeding grounds by the incoming tide, stream up the estuary to pastures new. It is best to arrive out there at high tide and, keeping to the path below the crest of the dunes, make for the hide. There, from its shelter, small numbers of great northern and red-throated divers have been seen. The rare black-throated diver has also been recorded from several locations elsewhere around the coast. Of the grebes you should see great crested, Slavonian and perhaps black-necked. Of ducks there should be mallard, teal, shelduck, wigeon – the last-named in hundreds, even thousands

Rhossili Bay   *H.E.G.*

Worms Head   *H.E.G.*

Weobley Castle   *H.E.G.*

Arthur's Stone, Cefn Bryn Common   *H.E.G.*

Ponies at Penclawdd   H.E.G.

Fordson Tractor, Burry Hill Farm   H.E.G.

Grey Heron, Llanrhidian Marsh   *H.E.G.*

Oystercatchers, Whiteford Point   *H.E.G.*

– with occasional pintail, shoveler, long-tailed duck and perhaps a few scaup. Special mention must be made of the eiders because these ducks are present here outside their normal distribution pattern in every month of the year. Up to now they have not bred. With the eiders you may also see a few red-breasted mergansers and the goosander, another sawbill, may also be seen from the hide but is more likely to be found on the rivers in the east of the county. Brent geese, mainly the dark-bellied variety, are regular in the estuary, in flocks of up to 700 each autumn and winter. The whitefronts that used to explore the Burry Inlet at night no longer appear to come. Instead, we get the occasional feral greylag goose and a few Canada geese.

The bulk of the waders consists of oystercatchers, with smaller flocks of grey and ringed plover. Often, especially in cold weather, sizeable flocks of golden plover, usually associated with lapwing, are to be found on the saltings between Landimore and Crofty and inland on suitable fields elsewhere in Gower. Otherwise the wader populations consist of dunlin, a few sanderling and cloud-like flights of knot, though not in such teeming numbers as formerly.

On the way back through the rushy marsh common snipe and jack snipe may be flushed from underfoot and grey herons will be fishing in the creeks that abound in the saltmarsh. Perhaps a kingfisher will be disturbed from its perch on the dyke. For a moment a peregrine, merlin or kestrel may put in an appearance, or a pair of buzzards will wheel overhead uttering mewing calls. Or, if you return through the plantation to Cwm Ivy, goldcrest, dun-nock, blackbird, song and mistle thrush, robin and wren can be added to your tally, winding up with pied wagtail and house sparrow in the cottage gardens and high hedgerows bordering the steep lane leading back to Llan-madoc.

In April or early May a walk from Rhossili to the Worms Head can yield encounters with both breeding and passage birds. Near the village will be newly arrived swallows and house martins. Sand martins, too, pass through the peninsula *en route* to their breeding grounds on the Loughor, Tawe, Clydach and Neath rivers. The first swifts will be about. On the walk to Kitchen Corner, stonechats, linnets and perhaps a yellow hammer will be watching from vantage points on top of gorse bushes and a whitethroat may bob up for a moment, to utter its scratchy song and vanish. Down on the causeway a belated purple sandpiper may be rummaging on the water's edge amongst the last few harlequin-coloured turnstones. If the tide is low enough to allow a visit to the rocky Crabart, you might see sandwich and other terns fishing there. Regrettably, numbers have decreased significantly in recent years. On the grassy slope of the Inner Head you may find the handsome wheatear. Where the northern face of the Outer Head falls vertically into the sea, guillemot, razorbill and kittiwakes will be seen on the breeding ledges. A few puffins may also be seen at the end of the Head, where they still breed in their traditional holes and shags may be seen hanging out their wings to dry. Their cousins, the cormorants, are found all along the coast, but have not bred in Gower since 1971. Fulmars however have established themselves in Gower since the 1950s and now regularly breed in many localities such as

Thurba Head and Lewes Castle. The salient position of the Worm, jutting right out away from the main coastline, makes it particularly inviting as a landmark or landing point for exhausted migrants: ring ouzels, wrynecks and yellow wagtails have been sighted there, to name but a few. Later in the summer, gannets from Grassholm dive on shoals of fish, and rafts of manx shearwater float gently in the swell. Rafts of common scoter, often numbering thousands of ducks, are present offshore from July into autumn and winter.

The National Nature Reserve at Oxwich may also be worth attention, particularly during the summer months. There is a hide near the village overlooking the South Serpentine Pond. From it you will see coot and moorhen, which breed, perhaps also a few pochard and tufted duck, though the duck population of the marsh seems to have suffered a serious decline. The alders along the pond banks are a favourite haunt of cetti's warbler, first recorded here in 1977 and now breeding regularly. Reed and sedge warblers with reed buntings can also be heard in the extensive phragmites beds and you may hear the secretive water rail uttering its weird squeals and grunts from close by. Oxwich is a good place for cuckoos, buzzards and tawny owls. The barn owl too may still be found quartering the marsh, as it does at other typical locations such as Fairwood and Clyne Commons; but the little owl prefers the Mewslade Valley and the vicinity of Gower's most famous bonecave at Paviland. Of the warblers, blackcap, chiffchaff and willow warbler are much in evidence in the woods which adjoin the marsh and stretch along the eastern side of Oxwich Point.

This rapid review would not be complete without a mention of Blackpill, in Swansea Bay, an excellent place to observe waders and gulls on a rising tide, emphasised by the discovery there of the first Mediterranean gull in 1970 and of an adult ring-billed gull in 1973, the latter being a first record for the UK. Both species are now regulars amongst the gull-flock and are also found at other localities around the coast. Bar-tailed godwits are present throughout the year, but the black-tailed godwit prefers the Burry Inlet, as do greenshanks and spotted redshanks. Blackpill is also a good place for ringed and grey plover and to look for rarer gulls such as Iceland, glaucous and little gulls. The occasional yellow-legged gull may be identified by experienced regular bird watchers.

So far we have mentioned some 125 species, considerably less than half of the 277 bird species recorded in the West Glamorgan area. So perhaps we should end on a high note by mentioning a few of the special birds that have been recorded in Gower recently. At Whiteford and the Burry Inlet: little egret and osprey; at Oxwich: bittern, hobby and great grey shrike; at Blackpill: avocet, curlew, sandpiper and little stint; elsewhere in Gower: waxwing (Sketty Park and West Cross), firecrest (Cheriton), yellow-browed warbler (Cheriton and Cwm Ivy), melodious warbler (Llanmadoc – only the second recorded in Glamorgan). The red kite is extending its breeding range and has been seen fairly regularly at the Cwm Clydach Reserve, Cwmdulais and Cilmaengwyn in the hinterland. It may soon breed in the peninsula itself.

This rapid review cannot be completed without acknowledgement to the Gower Ornithological Society and its excellent journal *Gower Birds*, together with the Gower Society, the National Trust, the Countryside Council for Wales, the Glamorgan Wildlife Trust, the Nature Conservancy Council and the Royal Society for the Protection of Birds, bodies who have spared no effort to conserve so much of Gower and its birdlife.

Amended and updated (1998) by Wyn Lewis
from the original by H. J. Hambury

GOWER PARISH CHURCHES
AND EARLY CHRISTIAN MONUMENTS

Introduction

The Christian Church has been present in Gower more or less continuously for somewhere around fifteen centuries; the ancient parish churches of this region are a direct link with the earlier church of this area. Many of the buildings are probably located on the same site as their early predecessors and some contain carved stones attesting to the antiquity of the Christian tradition there. Although the buildings themselves are ancient (generally about 700 years old), the sculptured or lettered stones are even older and date from the Celtic Church period (the Church before the introduction of the medieval Roman Church), their ages ranging from 800 to 1,500 years. A number of sixth century records in the 'Book of Llandaff' concern 'Llans' in Gower, some of which can still be positively identified.

In medieval days only three churches were under lay control, whilst the remainder were under ecclesiastical rule, split between monastic, episcopal and university ownership. After the dissolution of the monasteries some of the churches in monastic ownership passed to either lay impropriators or were retained by the Crown. This state of affairs ended in 1923 when the Church in Wales was disestablished and became a separate Province within the Anglican Communion.

It is not often realised that the number of medieval churches in Gower today is only about one half of those that are known to have existed. Among the ruined churches is the only site in Wales where direct evidence for a wooden church from the Celtic Church period has been found – this is Burry Holms chapel. Although it is the ancient parish churches which automatically spring to mind, Gower has a ruined chapel in Ilston Cwm, reputed to be the first Baptist meeting place in Wales, near the site of a pre-Reformation chapel.

Until recent times Gower was a relatively remote area and its churches do not display the splendour often found in other regions. This area was never wealthy and, as the Anglican Church in Wales lost its revenues on disendowment, the Gower churches are now dependent upon donations by parishioners and visitors for building preservation, etc.

Finally, the churches and their early monuments constitute a very rare continuum of visual evidence spanning over 1,500 years of Christianity. Most of the ancient stones are with their associated churches. However, the Roman altar from Loughor, with its Ogham (early Irish) writing, and the Gellionen Stone are in the Swansea Museum.

BISHOPSTON (Llandeilo Ferwallt) – St. Teilo   G.R. 57788936

The parish of Bishopston has within its bounds 'Llans' which date back to the earliest days of the Celtic Church (late 5th to early 6th centuries) and is identified in grants recorded in the *Book of Llandaff*.

In the days of the Celtic Church, it would appear to have been a minor 'mother church' attached to the great mother church at Llandaff, and remained part of the diocese of Llandaff until the rationalisation of diocesan boundaries in 1847. The present building probably grew out of an earlier chapel and took on its present extent during the 13th century. Within the chancel is an early piscina and the present font of 13th century vintage seems to be standing on one of an even earlier period. On the south side of the church are the remains of a medieval churchyard cross (possibly 14th century). The parish of Bishopston contained sanctuary land in medieval times, which was adjacent to the Backingstone Chapel above the Bishopston Valley.

CHERITON – St. Cadoc   G.R. 45059318

This church was built somewhere around the opening of the 14th century and is by far the most elegant and distinguished of the Gower medieval buildings. It is presumed that this church was built to replace one at Landimore which may have been affected by rising sea levels and encroachment on low-lying land. Both these churches were under the control of the Knights Hospitaller in Pembrokeshire. Between 1540 and 1923 the Lord Chancellor had responsibility.

The entrance into the church is a fine example of a doorway from the 'Decorated' period and within the chancel is a tub-shaped font of some antiquity. In the arch at the end of the nave can be seen the old rood loft entrance, which at one time could be approached up steps set in the wall of the choir.

ILSTON (Llanilltyd Gŵyr) – St. Illtyd   G.R. 55669034

It would appear from a reference in the 'Book of Llandaff' that a Christian cell was established here during the early 6th century called 'Llancynwalan'. Probably the early 'Llan' was abandoned and later re-established by, or transferred to, the 'mother church' at Llantwit Major and dedicated to St. Illtyd. A late 15th century Rector, William Smith, became a Bishop.

The present building grew out of an earlier chapel and probably took on its present form in the later middle ages. This parish was granted to the Knights Hospitallers, who retained it until 1540. Between 1540 and 1863 the Lord Chancellor had control, after which the parish passed into private hands.

A medieval bowl can be seen in the porch and in the chapel an unusual triangular-topped wall recess. In the nave is the pre-Reformation bell, which was removed from the tower in 1974.

LLANDEWI – St. David   G.R. 46018905

The origin of this church could be during the Celtic Church period and it appears to have been part of the estates belonging to the Bishop of St. David's from its founding until 1923.

There have been two major restorations (1876 & 1905) which, although retaining a few earlier features, removed more notable ones such a 17th century 'squire's pew'.

As far as the building itself is concerned, it has an unusual alignment in which the chancel deflects to the south. The reason for the misalignment can only be conjectured, although marking associated with the medieval 'scratch' sundial does suggest directional ignorance.

LLANGENNITH – St. Cenydd   G.R. 42879142

This church is specifically named in an early grant recorded in the *Book of Llandaff* and was reputedly founded by St. Cenydd in the 6th century. It was a 'Bangor' (or college) of sufficient importance for its destruction by the Vikings in the 10th century to be recorded in the *Chronicle of the Princes*. On the western wall of this church is an ornamental slab of 10th century vintage which is said to have covered St. Cenydd's tomb. Shortly before the Norman invasion, a church was consecrated here and five monks ordained by Bishop Herwald.

This was the largest of the churches on the Gower Peninsula and formed part of a Benedictine Priory under the Monastery of St. Taurin in Normandy. The farm building attached to the western end, together with this church, are all that remain of the Priory. In 1414 it was seized as an 'alien Priory' and was given to All Soul's College, Oxford in 1441.

St. Cenydd's Gravestone, Llangennith

A 13th century effigy can be seen near the font, and the previous existence of a rood loft is indicated by an elevated opening in the chancel arch.

LLANMADOC – St. Madoc   G.R. 43889345

From the presence of an early inscribed stone it can be presumed that the date of the original 'Llan' is prior to 550 A.D. The present building dates from the 13th century but underwent extensive restoration in 1865.

Set in the cill of the nave window is a lettered stone, which intriguingly displays Gallic as well as Irish characteristics in its formulation and dates from the period 450 to 550 A.D. In addition to this stone commemorating 'Advectus son of Guanus', there are in the west wall a crude pillar cross and a boundary marker, both of which come from the period 600-900 A.D. The present font is probably late Norman. A rood loft entrance can be seen in the chancel arch.

Pillar Cross Llanmadoc

This church was given to the Knights Templar in 1156, but on their suppression it passed, like many other of their churches, to the Knights Hospitallers in Herefordshire who retained it from 1309 until their dissolution in 1540. From 1540 until 1920 the incumbents were appointed by the Prince of Wales.

LLANRHIDIAN – St. Illtyd and St. Rhidian   G.R. 9679225

The date of the original 'Llan' may well be prior to 550 A.D., as at one time there was an inscribed stone (now lost) of early 6th century type in the vicinity. Also it is considered that 'Rhidian' is a corruption of 'Tryrulhid', the name of St. Illtyd's wife, and the lost stone verifies the antiquity of this site, thus adding credibility to this suggestion. The present building dates from the 13th century, but underwent extensive rebuilding in 1858. This church, together with a chapel at Walterston, was granted to the Knights Hospitaller in 1167, who retained them until 1540. From then on the incumbents were appointed by Lay Patrons until 1923.

On the tower roof is a large stone block, which is thought to have been used as a hearth for beacon fires. Within the porch is the mysterious 'Leper Stone' which is possibly a local variant of a 10th century Viking 'hog-back' tombstone, a type of monu-

The 'Leper' Stone, Llanrhidian

ment very rare in Wales. On the green outside are the remains of an 11th century wheel cross, known as the 'Pillory Stone'.

NICHOLASTON – St Nicholas   G.R. 51258842

As there is a church site beside the path leading down to Oxwich Bay, it is possible that the present site was not the first one. The present church's predecessor on the same site is thought to be of 14th century date and within the porch is a medieval tombstone. In 1894 the earlier building was almost completely rebuilt in the 'High Church' fashion of the Victorian period. The church interior is lavishly decorated in wood, alabaster and coloured marbles, although a few early fitments and features are present.

At one time Manselfield was attached to this parish and it is one of the few Gower churches where lay patronage existed in medieval times.

70

OXWICH – St. Illtyd   G.R. 50418612

This church stands on ground reputedly sacred since the 6th century. The present building is probably of 13th century construction but underwent restoration in the last century (circa 1890). A noted 17th century Rector of this parish was Hugh Gore who founded the Swansea Grammar School in 1682.

This is one of the few Gower Churches where medieval incumbents were appointed by lay patrons. For a not readily apparent reason, Nicholaston and Manselfield were part of Oxwich Parish.

The church contains monuments from the 13th and 14th centuries, one of which, the De La Mare effigy, is made from sand and plaster. When a portion was analysed, it was revealed that it was made from local sand which had been cemented together with a plaster and then covered with a painted plaster coat. Within the church is an ancient font and a 14th century bell, together with two grave-stones of the same period.

OYSTERMOUTH – All Saints   G.R. 61868800

There has been a church at Oystermouth since the days of the Celtic Church, as this church is mentioned by Nennius (9th century author). It is probable that there was a 'Llan' here before the 9th century and conceivable that the present building is on the site of the earlier 'Llan'. Beside or beneath the church was a Roman building with a tessellated floor, mosaic fragments from which have been found at various times. The north aisle of the present building was the original church until it was enlarged in 1860.

Following the Norman occupation of Gower, the church was granted to the Abbey of St. Peter at Gloucester. In 1367 the church was transferred to the Hospital of St. David in Swansea, who retained it until their suppression in 1540.

Within the church can be seen, amongst other objects, some fragments of Roman mosaic, an early font and a pillar piscina.

PENCLAWDD – St. Gwynour   G.R. 54869482

The ancient parish of Llanrhidian was divided in 1924 and its former 'chapel of ease' (Llanyrnewydd), serving Llanrhidian Higher, became the new Parish Church. In order to cater for the expanding Welsh-speaking population at Penclawdd, a mission church (St. David's) was built there in 1898 and it became a daughter church in the new parish.

By the late 1840s the original building, which may have been of medieval origin, had become so dilapidated that it was demolished and a new building erected in its place. Further building enlargement occurred in 1926.

PENMAEN – St. John the Baptist   G.R. 53188869

There is some evidence that this church was moved in the 13th century to make way for the medieval hunting park, Parc le Breos. Also, on the burrows is a besanded church, the function of which is unknown.

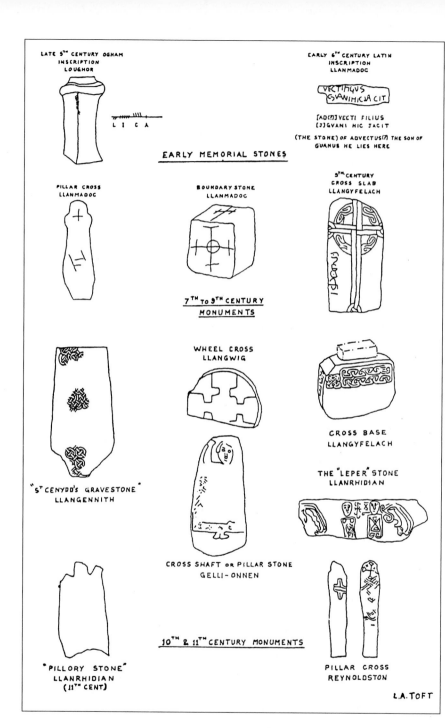

LATE 5TH CENTURY OGHAM
INSCRIPTION
LOUGHOR

L I C A

EARLY 6TH CENTURY LATIN
INSCRIPTION
LLANMADOC

VECTIHGVS
GVANIHICJACIT

[AD(?)]VECTI FILIUS
[J]GVANI HIC JACIT

(THE STONE) OF ADVECTUS(?) THE SON OF
GUANUS HE LIES HERE

EARLY MEMORIAL STONES

PILLAR CROSS
LLANMADOC

BOUNDARY STONE
LLANMADOC

9TH CENTURY
CROSS SLAB
LLANGYFELACH

7TH TO 9TH CENTURY
MONUMENTS

WHEEL CROSS
LLANGWIG

CROSS BASE
LLANGYFELACH

THE "LEPER" STONE
LLANRHIDIAN

"ST CENYDD'S GRAVESTONE"
LLANGENNITH

CROSS SHAFT OR PILLAR STONE
GELLI-ONNEN

"PILLORY STONE"
LLANRHIDIAN
(11TH CENT)

10TH & 11TH CENTURY MONUMENTS

PILLAR CROSS
REYNOLDSTON

L.A.TOFT

72

From the early 13th century, the church was under the Knights Hospitaller until their suppression. In 1854/5 the building was almost completely reconstructed, which left little of the original structure. It was during this restoration, however, that an unusual genealogical 17th century tombstone was discovered, and the lineage on it extends back to pre-Norman times. This memorial is now set on a wall. At one time the Manor of Paviland was part of this parish.

PENNARD – St. Mary   G.R. 56538873
The origin of this building is something of a mystery, since there are the remains of a church beside Pennard Castle and there are valid grounds for believing that the present early 13th century building could pre-date the ruined one.

This parish was granted by the Normans to the monastery of St. Taurin at Evreux in Normandy very early in the 12th century and they retained it until 1414, when it then came under the King's jurisdiction as an 'alien priory'. In 1441 it became part of the endowments of All Souls College, Oxford, who retained it until 1838. A letter sent circa 1535 by the then Vicar reports the besanding of the church beside the castle and is of great interest to historians.

At the church can be seen an ancient holy water stoup (now the font), a Jacobean pulpit and font cover, together with Laudian dog rails across the sanctuary, an ancient and unusual triangular-topped wall recess, and also early 13th century dog-tooth moulding on an external window.

PENRICE – St. Andrew   G.R. 49308795
This church is sited close to a Norman motte. The building is of cruciform plan and probably of 13th century date, but may incorporate earlier work. The church was under the Knights Hospitaller from the mid-12th century until their suppression. Later, lay patrons had control. Within the parish was medieval sanctuary land.

The building is noted for its very large porch, the inner door of which is hung on a free-standing structure. It is possible that this porch acted as a schoolroom during the 17th and 18th centuries. In 1893/4 the building was restored, but changes were not permitted.

PORT-EYNON – St. Cattwg   GR. 46668538
Although the present building dates from the 12th century, its origins are reputed to be in the 6th century. From the 12th century until their suppression this church was under the control of the Knights Hospitaller.

The earlier building was extensively renovated and enlarged in 1861, with a further restoration in 1901, but some of the ancient fitments still remain. Unusually this church does not have an east window.

In the churchyard is a marble statue commemorating the bravery and devotion to duty when three members of the crew of the local lifeboat 'Janet' were lost in a capsize whilst giving assistance to the steamship 'Dunvegan' in 1916.

REYNOLDSTON – St. George G.R. 47949003

This village and its church were reputedly founded by Sir Reginald de Breos, who died c.1221. It is unusual for churches before the 14th century to be dedicated to St. George and maybe the church had its original dedication altered. It was in private patronage prior to the Reformation.

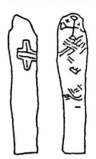

Pillar Cross
Reynoldston

The present building was extensively restored during the second half of the 19th century and little of its earlier work remains, apart from a blocked lancet window in the chancel. This church now houses the 10th century pillar cross which previously stood in a field beside the main road near Stouthall. The font is square and seems to have been made from a stalagmite. It is probably late Norman.

RHOSSILI – St. Mary G.R. 41668808

On the 'Warren' at the foot of Rhossili Down is the besanded church of Rhossili, which came under the control of the Knights Hospitaller during the 12th century.

The present church of Rhossili seems to be of 13th century date, but it has the only carved late 12th century Norman doorway in Gower. Above the doorway, however, is decoration typical of the early 13th century. On the doorway stonework is a medieval 'scratch' sundial and in the chancel a small 14th century 'leper' window can be seen. Within the church is a memorial to Petty Officer Edgar Evans who died on the expedition to the South Pole led by Captain Scott.

Luke Toft

COMMONS IN GOWER

Common land covers approximately 20% of the area of the Gower Area of Outstanding Natural Beauty. Some of these commons probably go back to prehistoric times when the better land was used for arable crops and the more distant, less fertile land used for communal pasture for livestock. There were few inhabitants, so there was little need to define these areas exactly or the inhabitants' rights. As populations increased, there was a need to limit usage of these communal areas and even before the Norman conquest there was the beginning of definite ownership of these lands and of certain rights granted to the local farmers.

After the Norman conquest of Gower, the land was held by the Marcher Lord or Lord Signeur, whose vassals held small manors. These vassals, in turn, sublet the land to tenant farmers and freeholders. The land was farmed on classic manorial lines, with arable strip fields, and communal grazing on the unenclosed poorer uplands, cliffs, marsh and heath. These grazing lands were the manorial waste or commons and the adjacent tenant farmers and freeholders were the commoners with rights of pasture (grazing of livestock), estover (use of small branches and underwood, including bracken), turbary (digging of turf or peat for fuel), piscary (fishing) and coire (use of surface stone).

Gower generally escaped the great enclosure movements of the 18th and 19th centuries. This was partly because some commons were poorly drained and unsuitable for agricultural development; but mostly because of the management policies of the two major landowners at that time – the Duke of Beaufort and the Penrice Estate. This may have been because both concentrated their efforts in exploiting the minerals to the East of Swansea. Port Eynon Moor was a notable exception, as it was enclosed in the late 17th century. There was also a small amount of encroachment onto common land by squatters and farmers especially after 1650. Farms were small, with low investment (tractors only came to Gower in 1934) and the landscape changed little.

The major use by Gower commoners was for grazing and each commoner had a 'stint' which allowed him a certain number of stock that could be grazed, depending on the size of his holding. In Gower, approximately 1½ acres of holding entitled the commoner to graze 1 beast or pony or alternatively 5 ewes with lambs. Many farms depended on this right for economic survival. Intercommoning rights were widespread around 1600, but at present this is restricted to ponies.

The other rights exercised nowadays in Gower are estover – mainly use of bracken for animal bedding – and coire.

Today, there are around 500 commoners in Gower, while the major landowners are the Duke of Beaufort (Somerset Trust), the National Trust and the City and County of Swansea. The commoners formed the Gower Commoners Association in 1947 to represent their interests. When the Commons Registration Act of 1965 was passed to resolve the many disputes over commons ownership and usage, they registered all their grazing land. Some common land has been lost as a result of this, as only land registered is now common land. For example, Gabriel Powell's Survey of 1764 refers to 16 acres of common land on Worms Head which is not on the current register.

Many of the commons are or contain Sites of Special Scientific Interest (SSSIs) or are Nature Reserves, while usage of others has decreased due to problems of livestock straying from the unenclosed commons onto roads and local gardens, dog worrying, disturbance by tourists, walkers and pony trekkers etc. The reduced grazing has led to deterioration of the vegetation (e.g. grass replaced by bracken and scrub).

Fencing and/or cattle grids may help, but are expensive and unless carefully designed can spoil the open aspect that the commons give to Gower. Hopefully, a recent (1998) lottery grant of £527,000 for the Gower Heathlands Group will allow additional grids, fencing and traffic calming measures to be installed, as well as scrub clearance.

It should be remembered that, in general, the public have no legal rights on commons except for rights of way. Exceptions include National Trust land, or where a special access deed has been agreed or, in the case of urban common, where there is a legal right to the public to use them for 'air and exercise'. There are nevertheless many other uses – golfing, walking, pony trekking, nature study, hang gliding, unauthorized grazing, wild fowling and car parking which are not all legal, but generally tolerated. The present Government is committed to legalize improved access to commons and it is to be hoped will do so soon.

The commons in Gower represent a wide range of habitats – salt marsh, inland commons, upland commons and sea cliff commons. Their diverse flora are described in the articles on 'Flowers and trees' and/or 'Seashore life', so are not included here.

A representative few of these commons are considered in more detail below:

1. Salt Marsh – Llanrhidian and Landimore Marshes

These salt marshes have been used for common land grazing for hundreds of years. A survey of Gower Anglicana in 1583 states: 'The lord and tennants of this Lordship may enter all commons as Llanrhidian Marsh and any other and have done tyme out of minde, without contradiction as farre as we know without lett or interruption'.

This is one of the largest commons on the Gower peninsula with an area of 1531 acres, belonging jointly to the National Trust and the Somerset Trust. The salt marsh is regularly washed by high tides, and the commoners graze sheep and ponies – around 3-4,000 ewes with lambs and several hundred ponies, together with a few cattle. Ponies walk in with the tide, though sometimes they will remain standing on slightly higher ground and wait till the tide recedes. Sheep do not move in with the tide, so have to be brought in or they will drown.

The marsh has a very characteristic flora, including cord grass, which was introduced to the area in 1935 to control erosion and trap silt. Cord grass is also grazed by ponies.

The Burry Inlet, of which this marsh is a part, holds the largest over-wintering population of waders and wild fowl such as oystercatchers, wigeon, knot, dunlin and lapwing and is of international significance.

The marsh is also used for cockle gathering and there have been cockle pickers since the earliest times. The cockles live in the soft and muddy sand of the estuary and are raked out and sieved to remove undersize cockles. After washing, the cockles are put into sacks. At one time, these were carried back on donkeys, later on horse drawn carts and more recently by tractors/ landrovers with trailers. The cockles are then boiled and as a result of recent Common Market legislation this is now carried out in process plants with strict quality and health requirements instead of the previous small back garden boilers.

2. Inland Commons – Welsh Moor, Fairwood and Clyne Commons

The soil of these commons is acidic, mostly glacial drift on millstone grit with many poorly drained areas.

Welsh Moor is notable for the marsh fritillary butterfly, whose caterpillars feed on the devil's bit scabious. Fairwood was donated to the Swansea City Council in 1935 with rights of general access and an aerodrome was constructed on it during the second world war. Many tons of hardcore had to be used on the boggy areas for this purpose and unfortunately two Bronze Age cairns or 'burchs' were destroyed. Clyne Common, being an urban common, has a general right of usage by the public for 'air and exercise' and also has a golf course. Fencing and cattle grids have been installed to restrain grazing animals and now that more stock is grazed, the deterioration of the land is beginning to be reversed.

3. Upland Commons – Cefn Bryn

This is the largest single common in peninsular Gower with an area of 2041 acres. It is owned by the Somerset Trust, the Penrice Estate and The National Trust.

It contains the second highest point in Gower as well as Arthur's Stone, a Neolithic tomb, and many other Bronze Age remains. The ridge is of old red sandstone giving an acid soil with fescue grass and bracken. The lower Northern slopes are rather waterlogged in parts and there are many bowl shaped depressions or 'sinks', a result of the collapse of caverns in the underlying limestone. Some of these sinks are water filled as they are clogged with glacial clay and form small pools. The largest of these is Broad Pool, a nature reserve with interesting flowers, insects and birds. There is also a dry, very large sink, Moormills, into which several small streams enter and disappear.

Grazing rights are recorded in the survey of 1583 of Gower Anglicana and the encroachment of two small-holders on Cefn Bryn is also mentioned. The right to 'cut furze and ferne for time out of mind' by the tenants of Walterston manor is given in a survey of 1689. Sheep, cattle and ponies still graze the common today, but not as many as earlier because of problems of visitors and lack of fencing and, therefore, the pasture is deteriorating. Recently some cattle grids have been installed and hopefully further work will reverse this trend.

An old track, Talbot's Way, runs along the ridge of this common with extensive views in all directions. The Ordnance Survey made use of this for surveying and erected two triangulation point pillars in 1938. A view point near the main road on the ridge above Reynoldston gives the direction of and distance to major features visible from this point. A commemorative plaque at the East end of the ridge records the inauguration of the Gower Way, a path from Rhossili, along Cefn Bryn to Penlle'r castell in the far North of inland Gower. Rhossili Down, Llanmadoc Down, Hardings Down and Ryer's Down all fall into the same group as Cefn Bryn and have many similarities.

4. Sea Cliff Commons – Pennard Cliffs and Pennard and Penmaen Burrows

These are all on the South coast of Gower, where the tops of the dramatic carboniferous limestone cliffs are covered by thin, well drained soils. Many areas are covered by windblown sand from the great storms of the 14th-16th centuries, forming extensive dunes or burrows. Most of this area is owned by the National Trust, but Pennard Burrows belongs to Pennard Golf Club.

The cliff top pastures here are now not used except for a little grazing. Rabbits are returning and ponies graze the inland besanded area of Pennard, which is now grass covered and a popular golf course.

The area is rich in prehistoric and medieval history. There are caves in the Pennard cliffs with remains of prehistoric animals (see Gazetteer entries for Bacon Hole and Minchin Hole). A Neolithic burial chamber can be found on Penmaen Burrows, while an Iron Age promontory fort, one of many on the South Gower coast, is situated on the cliff edge at High Pennard. There are, in addition, remains of Norman castles at the eastern extremity of Penmaen and a little inland at Pennard as well as scanty remains of old churches near each castle. The ring work and wooden tower castle at Penmaen was abandoned in the 13th century and replaced by the stone built Pennard Castle. This latter castle and the two churches were in turn abandoned after the besanding already referred to. Traditionally, small settlements near these buildings were also overwhelmed by sand.

Rabbits, introduced by the Normans, were farmed in artificial warrens called pillow mounds and provided fresh meat in winter. Such a mound can be seen on Penmaen Burrows near the old castle.

In conclusion, the many and varied commons of Gower will hopefully continue to serve, inspire, educate and interest local inhabitants and visitors alike for many generations to come.

Albert White

A List of Commons on the Gower Peninsula
(see map on page 120)

Rhossili Downs and Cliffs	Mynydd Bach y Cocs
Hardings Down and Pitton Cross	Pennard Cliffs and Burrows
Ryers Down	Fairwood and Clyne Commons (Partly)
Llanmadoc Hill and Tankeylake Moor	Bishopston Valley
	Barlands Common
Llanrhidian and Landimore Marshes	Penmaen and Nicholaston Burrows
	Slade Cliffs
Llanrhidian Hill and the Common	Common and Overton Cliffs
The Wern and the Rallt	Newton and Summerland Cliffs
Cefn Bryn	Bracelet Common
Pengwern	Middle Head, Mumbles
Welsh Moor, Bryn and Forest	Langland Cliffs

CONSERVATION
and the GOWER A.O.N.B.

Gower is a happy accident of geological forces, climatic conditions and human enterprise: a harmonious blend of landscape, nature and history. This *'rare patch of the Earth's surface'*, as Wynford Vaughan Thomas called it, is a rich mix of natural scenic beauty, farmed landscape and diverse flora.

Until relatively recently, the peninsula was protected by its comparative inaccessibility. In the nineteenth century, more trade was done with Cornwall than with Swansea; and up until the first World War, and even beyond, Gower remained to a large extent separate from its urban neighbours. Only in the late 1920s were roads improved sufficiently to allow motor vehicles, and there were few of those. Lady Blysthwood, who ruled Penrice from 1920 to 1949, and who has been described as *'benevolent despot of two-thirds of the Gower landscape'*, saw no reason for change. It was only after her death, and that of Admiral Heneage-Vivian in 1952, that the large estates of Penrice, Clyne and Le Breos were eventually broken up. David Rees, founder member of the Gower Society, recently recalled the early 1950s, when *'the peninsula was in general isolated and deserted in a way that seems almost unimaginable today'*. Much of Gower had remained unspoilt, not through any positive intention to conserve it, but because of a *'policy of stagnation'*.

Suddenly Gower's vulnerability was exposed, and exploitation became a serious and urgent reality. The Gower Society had been established early in 1948, mainly to study·Gower and to produce a journal of its findings. Within a few months, however, the role of conservationist was thrust upon it when plans were announced for a Butlin's Holiday Camp at Rhossili. The campaign to prevent the 'despoilation of this untouched tip of Gower' was so successful that the Society became the natural leader in campaigns over the next few years to prevent the destruction of Oxwich Castle keep, the felling of Crawley Woods, the erection of a 150m. radar mast on Rhossili Down and the establishment of a shell-testing range in the Burry Estuary.

The protection of natural isolation had gone for ever. The development of the U.K. motorway system in the second half of the twentieth century and the massive increase in car ownership, coupled with widespread tourism publicity, have put twenty million people within four hours travelling time of Gower. On a fine summer's day 50,000 day trippers will join the 30,000 holiday makers enjoying an environment that they might be helping to destroy. While we delight in sharing Gower with those who appreciate beauty, peace and tranquillity, there is a danger from too many feet, too many wheels and too many hooves. The increased crowdedness, the litter, the worn-down look are familiar signs of excessive human pressure. The fundamental question is, as Goodman asked in the first edition of this *Guide*, whether we are skilful enough in managing our environment to balance the many purposes of Gower without subjecting it to pressures it cannot sustain.

The designation, in 1956, of peninsular Gower as the first Area of Out-

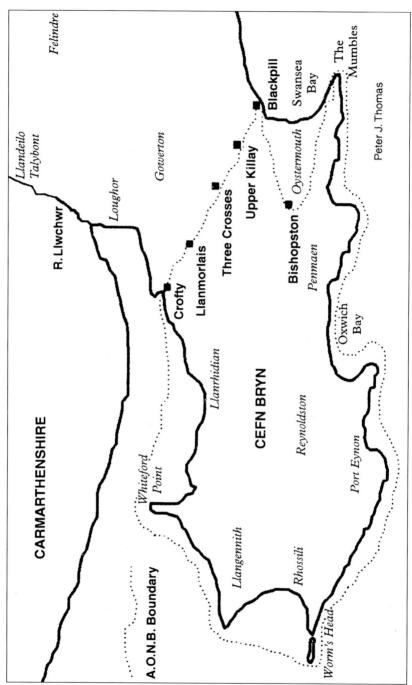

Area of Outstanding Natural Beauty (A.O.N.B.) Boundary.

CARMARTHENSHIRE

A.O.N.B. Boundary

Felindre

Llandeilo Talybont

R.Llwchwr

Loughor

Gowerton

Blackpill

Swansea Bay

The Mumbles

Peter J. Thomas

Upper Killay

Three Crosses

Llanmorlais

Crofty

Oystermouth

Bishopston

Penmaen

Llanrhidian

CEFN BRYN

Reynoldston

Oxwich Bay

Whiteford Point

Llangennith

Rhossili

Port Eynon

Worm's Head

standing Natural Beauty (A.O.N.B.) in the whole of the United Kingdom was welcomed by almost everyone. Jenkin John, Chairman of the County Planning Committee, announced that '*In Gower, private interest will take second place to public interest*'. But the designation was a two-edged sword: while it gave status to the area, it gave only minimal protection, and increased the pressures from both visitors and 'developers'.

Gower is unique in the U.K. In its mild climate and diverse habitat, upwards of one thousand species of plant flourish, including a dozen types of orchid and the yellow whitlow grass, a plant found in the wild nowhere else in Britain. The AONB comprises almost exactly half of the 38,000 hectares of the old lordship (and present-day City and County of Swansea). There are four National Nature Reserves, including the RAMSAR site on the Burry Estuary, seventeen other nature reserves, twenty-seven Sites of Special Scientific Interest and fifty-five hectares of Heritage Coastline. Add to this the wealth of pre-historic remains, including one of the earliest human skeletons found in Britain, burial cairns, Bronze Age dolmens and Iron Age forts, together with eight Norman castles, a host of churches and a fair sprinkling of domestic buildings – and the richness of Gower becomes apparent. The delicate balance that produces such an abundance of life needs not only protection, but positive and sympathetic management.

Management is essential. Left to themselves, buildings decay and fall into ruin; woodlands deteriorate, commons turn into scrublands. The south Gower limestone cliffland exemplifies the problems of management: in some parts towards the west, overgrazing by sheep has led in hot dry summers to scorched, almost bare earth, which, when the rain has returned, has been colonised by plantain rather than grass. To the east, increased human and dog population has led to farmers withdrawing their sheep from the cliffs, with the result that now some parts are almost impassable because of bramble, gorse and bracken.

Management involves choices. Choices between what is to be protected and what is to be destroyed, what is to be encouraged and what discouraged. What principles direct our priorities? When only one domain is under consideration, the answer is relatively straightforward: we favour the rare rather than the commonplace, and variety above monotony. In a choice between the fen orchid and the dandelion, the fen orchid will always have priority. We clear bracken in the hope of halting its monocultural progress, and allowing the regeneration of the cowslips, bluebells and campions that have been choked out by the bracken's absolute domination of its habitat. The same principles of rarity and variety apply to archaeological and historical remains, but circumscribed by the knowledge that, once lost, such remains can never be resurrected.

The problems arise when there is a conflict of priorities between one domain of interest and another; between rock-climbers and nesting kittiwakes; walkers and eroded footpaths; housebuilders and visual amenity. Compromise might be possible: the climbers can be allowed the cliffs for nine months, and the birds given priority for three; footpaths can be redirected, if only temporarily, to allow recovery or sympathetic strengthening;

a change of position or of construction material can change a house from being a blot on a beautiful landscape to an acceptable, even attractive part of the vista.

An AONB is a particularly attractive area in which to live, and consequently a particularly profitable area in which to erect houses. The *Financial Times* once commented on how unfortunate it was for speculators that Gower had been declared an AONB. Even so, far too many buildings have got through the planning net, sometimes as a result of planning approvals given years ago, sometimes as 'agricultural dwellings'. New housing, if it is not to be damaging to the environment, needs to be strictly controlled in amount, location and design. It needs to meet a social or economic need of the community and make a positive contribution to the village scene. Need, not greed, must be the criterion. Other developments, be they tourist or commercial, must also be of a scale and type that recognises the sensitivity of the AONB. There is a real danger of creeping suburbanization: overhead power and telephone cables, telecommunications masts, unnecessary kerbing of roads, a proliferation of large and badly designed signs advertising 'attractions' – all these can subtly alter the experience of being in the countryside. And most of them are unnecessary.

The rural landscape of Gower owes a great deal to its combination of commons and small fields, some of medieval origin. While changes have occurred, the majority of farmers are still Gower men and proud of it. On their family farms, hedges, banks, ponds, copses and marshy hollows have survived as part of a traditional farmed landscape. Despite increased pressures on farmers, every effort should be made to retain these traditional features and to seek support for the farmers to enable them to do so. As Michael Haines has pointed out: '*For the individual farmer, food and recreation are goods he can sell; but the public goods of landscape, wildlife habitat and quality of environment are a by-product for which he cannot charge*'. If support for food subsidies declines, and with it the farmers' income, then the only way to maintain those public goods in sensitive areas such as AONBs might be a long-term environmental support system, such as was trialled in Gower with the Tir Cymen scheme and is being extended across Wales. Economic laws do not recognise AONB boundaries, and the greatest protection we can give to our landscape is to ensure a strong and viable, local farming community.

Conservation is not about maintaining the *status quo*; still less about returning to some artificially idyllic, pre-industrial revolution dream. It is about managing change in such a way that allows the essential character of Gower – its natural scenic beauty, its farmed landscape, its history and its diverse flora – to remain. We shall not go far wrong if we recognise the need to balance conservation with the legitimate well-being of the community, without allowing the short-term financial gain of the few to be attained at the long-term expense of the heritage that belongs to us all. If we remember that Gower was not given to us by our fathers, but lent to us by our children, we shall not let them, or it, down.

Malcolm Ridge

DIALECT

(*Editors' Note:* Even on the Peninsula these days it is unusual to hear the old dialect of Gower. An abridged version of the original article by Mr. Horatio Tucker which appeared in the earlier editions has been retained in this 1999 edition. It is hoped that it might foster a renewed interest in the local methods of expression).

The Gower dialect has been neglected by scholars in the past, and consequently many old words have died out without having been recorded. Separation from the parent speech for many centuries has resulted in characteristics peculiar to Gower and wide variations in the form of words of West Country origin.

The features common to Gower and South Pembrokeshire speech are due either to their common origin or to their mutual contact with Welsh speaking peoples. The most obvious differences are the result of the many years of isolation from each other and from their parent West Country dialect.

Many English words that have changed their meaning over the years still retain their earlier meanings in the Gower dialect. Words such as '*nice*' meaning 'fastidious' and '*frightened*' meaning 'astonished'.

Typical of many dialect words peculiar to Gower, but still recognisable even in their changed form with West Country words, are '*blonkers*' meaning 'sparks' and '*nestletrip*' for the smallest pig in a litter.

Words have been retained that are common to the Scottish, Northern England and Wexford dialects, whereas they have disappeared in the south. Dialect words such as '*tite*' meaning 'overturn' or '*keek*' for 'peep' were doubtless widely distributed in ancient times, but now associated only with Scotland and Northern England, have survived in Gower.

Some variations in dialect words have resulted from differences in local trade or landscape. '*Dumbledarry*' is widely distributed across the Peninsula as the name for a cockchafer, but in South Gower the name for a cockchafer is '*oakwib*' and was probably introduced during the heyday of the limestone trade with Devon.

Other dialect words are limited in use to one parish only such as '*bumbagus*' which is the Oxwich name for a bittern, a bird once common on Oxwich Marshes.

Abriged & revised by
D. Strawbridge & P. J. Thomas
from the original by Horatio Tucker

Footnote: After completing the above article the authors were informed of the following book: *Gowerland & Its Language* by Robert Penhallurick (1994) priced at £18. Details are available from the author at the Department of English, University of Wales, Swansea SA2 8PP.

FARMING IN GOWER

Editors' Note: *The article 'Farming' which appeared in earlier editions of 'A Guide to Gower' and is reproduced here, was written by the late Ernest Richards, born in Rhossili in 1907, who farmed at Horton from 1934, who held high office in the NFU and on various Parliamentary Committees. For this sixth edition we are pleased to be able to include an update, 'The Changed Face of Gower Farming', written by another active Gower farmer, Christopher Beynon.*

Pitt Farm

Farming

A look over the shoulder at the recent history of Gower farming will immediately establish the inter-war years, or more precisely the twenty years 1922-42, as the period of the swiftest change. Up to that period the pattern here, unlike areas that had been opened up by rail communication two generations previously, had been virtually unchanged for a very long time. Absence of mechanised transport had dictated a way of farming where the product walked to market, and batches of fat cattle and sheep were to be seen being driven to Swansea every Saturday throughout the winter: from the far end of the peninsula a start would be made on the previous evening and the cattle would rest at Penrice Home Farm overnight.

The coming of the motor lorry meant that crops could be grown for sale and whereas formerly the summer was spent in producing and storing crops for winter-feeding, from now on part of the summer production, notably potatoes, swedes and green crops were increasingly grown for direct sale off the farms.

About 1930, came the realisation of the favoured position of the peninsula as a comparatively frost-free area. This coincided with the introduction of new improved cropping varieties of early potatoes, and the result was that early potatoes became an important contribution to most farm incomes, especially in the coastal strip. This maintained the arable acreage in Gower at a time when the rest of the country was going back to grass very quickly indeed, and this nurtured the traditions and skills of crop farming, so that when the wartime policy of 'plough for plenty' posed many problems and brought howls of protest from many parts of the country, Gower farmers took this in their stride. The late '30s saw milk production get under way. In this development Gower lagged behind the rest of Glamorgan, for although the absence of railways had been overcome, lack of water supply was a retarding factor. The availability of piped water and the establishment of organized milk marketing were the two factors which give impetus to dairying after 1936.

The other major change was, of course. the mechanisation of farming. This took place at the same time as it did over the rest of the country and the pattern is so typical that it calls for no special comment. The present picture is one of larger fields, more corn growing and, on the open commons, many more ponies. Urban affluence has brought with it a tremendous demand for riding ponies. Farm houses and buildings are increasingly taking on a new look with general purpose-type buildings, which are so suitable for modern farming methods and which after a few years of weathering will merge harmoniously into the landscape.

A thought or two about the future. Gower is increasingly becoming the playground of an industrial hinterland and beyond (fortunate indeed to have such a playground!). We have to live with the problems this will bring. and provided the visitor observes the elementary rules of good behaviour. There is no reason why a good time should not be had by all. Finally the Royal Commission's report on common land is now being implemented by Act of Parliament. Since half the acreage of Gower is common land, changes in its productivity could have some effect on future production patterns. The legislation recognizes the amenity value of what the Commission's report calls 'the last of the country's uncommitted land', but this need not prejudice the improved utilisation of these areas nor rob them of their peculiar character and charm.

Ernest Richards

The Changed Face of Gower Farming
Since the late Ernest Richards' excellent article above, Gower farming has changed considerably. Very few people from outside Gower have come here to farm but whenever land has been sold, mainly due to retirements, it has been bought by neighbours and amalgamated into larger holdings albeit retaining the 'family farm' structure.

Dairying in Gower which had become an enterprise on most farms is now in the hands of fewer, more specialised units. Economic herd size has risen so that 100 cows is almost a minimum viable unit. Strict control of milk production and sale has meant that delivery of local farm milk around the villages is a thing of the past and all the milk is handled in bulk by the national dairies.

There is still a fairly large acreage of cereals grown in Gower. Technology has increased yields considerably over the past 50 years but rising costs and reduced returns are beginning to make cereal growers worried about their future viability. Most mixed farmers are still growing small acreages for home use but the need for larger growers to invest heavily in better drying, handling and storage of grain will probably speed the process of fewer farms growing larger acreages at the expense of their smaller neighbours. Very few buyers, each representing large multi-national companies, now only want to purchase quality grain, produced and stored to the requirements of the latest current legislation.

Beef production, so long a backbone of the relatively small family farms in Gower, is very much in decline. The BSE crisis and confusion of the early 1990s, which saw a ban of exports of beef from UK to the rest of the world, and an underlying reduction in consumption within the home market has reduced demand and very much reduced profitability in this sector. It is very difficult to see any improvement within the near future and one can only expect a continued decline in this traditional enterprise.

Sheep numbers in Gower probably have never been so high. The Gower climate of mild winters and early springs together with adequate moisture during the summer months means that production of grass is as cheap in Gower as anywhere in the world except perhaps New Zealand. The rough grazing provided by the common land and cliff grazing, which together amount to more than half the area of land devoted to agriculture in Gower, are ideal for sheep production and we can only presume that lamb production will thrive into the future.

Perhaps the greatest change in Gower farming over the last 20 years has been the increase in horticultural production. Specialist early potato growing, which began in the late 1930s and has thrived in the post war years, is still a very important part of Gower farm production. The real change has come in the area of green crop vegetables, which has increased considerably. The Gower climate is ideal for year round production and the vegetable crop fits in well on the family farm. Marketing of quality potatoes and green crops into the demanding shop and supermarket trade is a very particular skill. Government capital input in the form of grants to aid farmers marketing has allowed the establishment of 'Gower Growers', who control and market most Gower farmers' products thereby allowing daily access to quality markets.

The establishment of 'Sites of Special Scientific Interest' (SSSIs) and, recently, more positive management of Gower commons is undoubtedly going to change large areas of Gower. We are all becoming more aware of our environment and the need to look ahead to ensure the long term future of mankind. To positively manage these areas to improve their wellbeing will be difficult if not impossible, but we hope that today's scientists will succeed.

Gower agriculture from the days of Ernest Richards' review has changed and on the whole prospered. The 1947 Agricultural Act and, subsequently, the administration and control from Brussels has meant that agriculture has been controlled by politicians for more than 50 years. At the start of that period we were desperately short of food, now we have overproduction of food throughout the developed countries of the World. Politicians have controlled agricultural production by financial manipulation throughout this period of time and one can only assume they will wish to keep control in the future. The future of Gower and of Gower farmers lies with these politicians.

Christopher Beynon

FLOWERS AND TREES IN GOWER

Gower owes much of its designation as the first A.O.N.B. in 1956 to its indigenous flora and fauna. It is an area of subtle contrasts – a microcosm of diverse environmental types. Here, you will find moorland, heath, farmland, cliffs, sand dunes, pebble and sandy beaches, woodland, fresh-water and estuarine habitats.

To fully appreciate its flora, take a small x 10 hand lens with you on your walks. Having seen the flower structure in close-up, with its central carpel and surrounding stamens, the complexity of its petals with their venation and markings, you will view flowers in an entirely different light. In a short article, it is impossible to list every plant you can find – this is just a 'taster' to the enormous variety to be found.

A comparatively small area of Gower (some 7%) is woodland, dominated by oak and ash, with some wych elm and sycamore but beech is not wide-spread; in Bishopston Valley, you can find the uncommon small four leafed lime. The under-storey is likely to support holly, hawthorn, spindle, field maple, hazel and dogwood. Damp areas on commons will have birch; Oxwich has numerous alders and willows. Trees in Parkmill are excellent testimony to the pollution-free air, as they sport extensive lichen growth. Spring sees the woodland floor covered with dog's mercury followed by bluebells, wild garlic (or ramsons), primroses, violets, bugle, wood anemones. This is a scenic and scented splendour of riches, amongst which you may spot red campion, tutsan, enchanter's nightshade, herb bennet, wood sanicle and daffodils (in some cases, the double form). Many woods hold stands of the bushy butcher's broom, where 'leaves' are actually side branches, and true leaves are tiny scales. It has inconspicuous greenish flowers on the 'leaves' which are followed by red berries – both may be present together. The diligent searcher may find toxic herb paris, pale chlorophyll-free parasitic toothwort (a member of the broomrape family), early purple orchid, stinking hellebore, Welsh poppy, and both caper and wood spurge. Common polypody fern is abundant on trees – it also grows on the ground. Ferns thrive in shady moist areas. The stinking iris (smell its leaves where they are damaged) grows beneath the pines on the sandy ground at Whiteford.

Coastal areas are subjected to salt-laden air and strong westerly winds which the plants have to tolerate. Trees show characteristic 'wind pruning' where exposed. Coastal grassland has spring squill, orchids, dovesfoot cranes-bill, wood sage. Isle of Man cabbage and sea bindweed can be found behind Pobbles beach in the valley. Gorse and blackthorn are typical scrub plants amongst foxglove, salad burnet and carline thistle. Common and hoary rock rose, rock sea spurrey, wild thyme and basil thyme, common milkwort (pink, blue and white forms), devil's bit scabious, and scarlet (and blue and pink forms) pimpernel jostle for supremacy. On the headlands, those with a keen eye can locate diminutive autumn lady's tresses. Vertical rock faces may have the Gower speciality, yellow whitlow grass (easily seen on Pennard castle), wall pellitory, wall saxifrage and scurvy grass species. Beneath the cliffs and above the shore, you can find sea beet, golden samphire and rock samphire.

The dune systems can be extensive. Oxwich and Whiteford have creeping willow with its frothy seed heads, wild privet, dewberry, burnet rose (which may have galls of the gall wasp) and stands of hemp agrimony, so beloved by insects. Isolated pines and yews are self-sown, and there are some established birch spinneys. Oxwich has an extensive sward of red campion, bluebells and cowslips in Spring – an inspiring sight. In recent years, grazing has effectively curtailed scrub development in some areas, allowing ground flora to flourish. Dune edges on the seaward side are dominated by the sand-consolidating marram grass. Further inland, biting stonecrop carpets its yellow swathes, together with wild thyme, bloody cranesbill, rest harrow (some may have white flowers), sea centaury, bird's foot trefoil, yellow rattle, yellow-wort, red bartsia, with specimens of viper's bugloss and sea holly, some bee orchids and abundant evening primrose and pyramidal orchids. In the damper dune slacks, there is creeping variegated horsetail, early marsh and southern marsh orchids, common twayblade, marsh helleborine, marsh pennywort, and round-leaved wintergreen. The sight of the dune (Welsh) gentian thrusting from the sand is one not to be missed in late summer. At Whiteford, the diligent may spot the rare and diminutive fen orchid. In the dunes, you may also spot the peculiar saprophytic, strikingly yellow-coloured yellow birdsnest. Oxwich has a large area of reedswamp, fen and willow carr, where you can find yellow iris, ragged robin, purple loosestrife, marsh cinquefoil, marsh bedstraw, water lilies, bulrush, common reed, reedmace, common sedge and water dock. The water also holds the insectivorous bladderwort.

Broadpool, near Cillibion, is famous for its fringed water lily – a yellow delight in summer. Farm ponds and damper areas can also show, in and around their margins, extensive flora, e.g. broad-leaved pondweed, water starwort, purple loosestrife, angelica, toxic hemlock water-dropwort, water mint, brooklime, water forget-me-not, water bistort, water crowfoot (both large-flowered and ivy-leaved), common fleabane, spiked water milfoil, giant horsetail and sometimes bogbean.

The northern salt-marsh has short-cropped, extensively grazed vegetation, which in early autumn is a purple haze due to sea lavender. The flora can include sea plantain, sea rush, thrift, spear-leaved orache, sea mayweed, red fescue, buck's horn plantain and sea wormwood; in drier areas, yellow horned poppy grows. Edible Salicornia (glasswort) is well worth a nibble! Below Llanmadoc, there is abundant yellow iris and marsh mallow. Ricegrass (*Spartina townsendii*) continues its stealthy advance, notably in Swansea Bay.

Commons cover large areas of Gower and, at first glance, may appear to be bracken-covered only, but they repay closer scrutiny. In the wetter parts, you will find cotton grass, common rush, cross-leaved heath, the insectivorous sundew, bog asphodel with its bright golden starry flowers and marsh marigold; elsewhere, there is gorse, lousewort, tormentil, delicate pale pink bog pimpernel, marsh St. John's wort, lesser skullcap, fragrant meadowsweet, and cuckoo flower. The royal fern is a rarer specimen and there are excellent specimens between Sluxton and Llangennith. Upland areas, on the moist peat, have heather and bilberry but tend to be dominated by purple moor grass. Pink-flowered English stonecrop flourishes on the drier rocky areas.

Farmland can still produce corn marigold (Paviland area), field pansies and common spotted orchids (Henllys area). Arable weeds such as ramping and common fumitory, corn spurrey, field bindweed, groundsel, numerous thistle species, scentless mayweed, eyebright and silverweed often edge the crops. Dry stone walls support numerous lichens plus the ubiquitous wall pennywort, ivy-leaved toadflax, dwarf maidenhair spleenwort, various cranesbill species, and rue-leaved saxifrage. Hedge banks, away from council-manicured verges, support colourful successive populations including the herb, majoram, field scabious, blue meadow cranesbill, Jack-by-the-hedge, wild arum, colts-foot, greater stitchwort, hedge parsley, etc. all topped by clematis, honeysuckle, black bryony and dog rose.

No attempt has been made to deal in detail with the non-flowering plants which form such a vital, but less attention-stealing, part of Gower's rich floral tapestry (both on the shore and inland). There are abundant specialised texts to help identify the many species which Gower supports; some relevant books are mentioned in the Guide's 'Book List'.

Ruth Ridge

Devil's Bridge, Worms Head

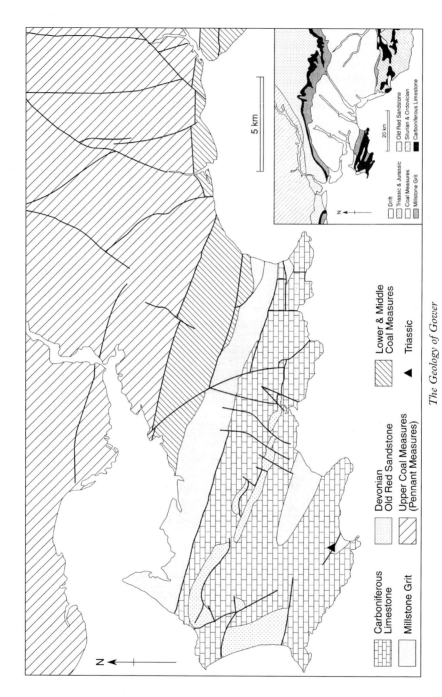

The Geology of Gower

Carboniferous
Limestone

Millstone Grit

Devonian
Old Red Sandstone

Upper Coal Measures
(Pennant Measures)

Lower & Middle
Coal Measures

▲ Triassic

5 km

Drift

Triassic & Jurassic

Coal Measures

Millstone Grit

Old Red Sandstone

Silurian & Ordovician

Carboniferous Limestone

20 km

N

THE
GEOLOGY
AND
SCENERY
OF GOWER

Great Tor, Tor Bay

The rocks of Gower formed between 400 and 300 million years ago in the Devonian and Carboniferous periods of geological time. The landscape then was quite unlike today's. There were no hills and cliffs, no Bristol Channel or Burry Estuary, and no Coalfield. Southern Britain lay on the edge of a fragment of the earth's crust (a tectonic plate) just south of the equator, where it experienced a tropical climate.

The oldest rocks on Gower are Devonian conglomerates (fossilised gravels) and sandstones known as the Old Red Sandstone. They were the alluvial deposits of large rivers that flowed into the Rheic Ocean south of Wales during the Devonian period. The conglomerates with their pebbles of white quartz and red jasper can be seen along the ridges of Rhossili Down and Cefn Bryn. Early in the Carboniferous period a clear tropical sea flooded the area that would become South Wales. It teemed with life, and the shells of animals that lived on the sea-bed form the fossil-rich Carboniferous Limestone. This can be examined along much of the South Gower coast, and the fossils include corals, brachiopods (sea-shells) and crinoids ('sea-lilies'). Muds washed into the sea later in the Carboniferous period have hardened into the shale-rich Millstone Grit. This is poorly exposed, but can be seen in stream beds on Barland Common and on the foreshore at West Cross. Later, equatorial forests colonised deltas similar to that of the Mississippi today. Peat layers that formed in the swamps have been compressed into the coal seams of the Coal Measures. Coal-mining has long gone from Gower, but the coal seams and their associated sandstones and shales can be examined in the former Killay brick-pit in the Clyne Valley Country Park, where fossil mussels have been found in the shales. The deltas were later replaced by large rivers whose sandy deposits make up the Pennant Measures at the top of the Coal Measures. From the oldest Old Red Sandstone at the base of the rock succession to the youngest Pennant Measures at the top, the pile of rocks that form Gower is over 4,000 metres (2.5 miles) thick!

The once-horizontal rock layers are now bent and broken. On Gower they have been crumpled like a concertina, and can be seen standing on end at Great Tor, or bent into folds at Bracelet Bay and West Cross foreshore. At the very end of the Carboniferous period, movements of the tectonic plates closed the Rheic Ocean. The continents on either side of it collided, squeezing the rocks in between and throwing up a range of mountains, in the same way that the Alps have more recently been formed by the collision of Africa with Europe. The structures formed by this Variscan deformation include the major down-warp (syncline) of the Coalfield with a trend from west to east, and a series of synclines and anticlines (upfolds) trending northwest to southeast on the Gower peninsula.

In the long period that followed the Variscan deformation, erosion removed much of the rock succession. Erosion tries to produce a level surface but is confounded by the varying toughness of the rocks. Ironically, the oldest rocks – the Old Red Sandstone – which lie at the bottom of the rock pile, form the highest ground, where they emerge in the cores of anticlines. This is because the tough conglomerates resist erosion. Easily-eroded Millstone Grit shales are preserved along synclines and correspond to valleys or, at the coast, the major bays of Oxwich and Port-Eynon. Likewise, the shale-rich lower part of the Coal Measures underlies the Burry Estuary and Swansea Bay. The tough Pennant Measures form the high ground of Three Crosses, Dunvant, Townhill and Kilvey Hill. Overlying the Pennant Measures, however, the youngest Coal Measures in South Wales – the Grovesend Beds – are again shale-rich and easily eroded, forming a belt of lower ground from Llanelli to Gorseinon.

The Variscan deformation also broke the rocks along fractures and faults, many trending north-south. At the coast these have been eroded to form the many smaller bays like Three Cliff or Caswell, and erosion inland has formed narrow valleys like Mewslade. Solution of limestone by water widens joints and bedding planes allowing water to flow underground, so across the outcrop of the Carboniferous Limestone these valleys are often dry and associated with caves, as in the Bishopston Valley and Green Cwm. Fractures in the limestone are commonly filled with crystals of white calcite, and in places this is accompanied by metal ores, that have been worked for iron at Mumbles, and lead in the Bishopston Valley.

The Gower landscape can be envisaged simply as a series of steps, or platforms. Much of Gower lies at about 60m above sea-level, underlain by Carboniferous Limestone, while the highest points on the Old Red Sandstone are at similar heights on Rhossili Down (193m), Cefn Bryn (188m) and Llanmadoc Hill (186m). The reasons for the relief of Gower have been debated for many years. Patches of red mudstone in south Gower probably accumulated in the hot desert environment of the Triassic period, some 220 million years ago. The mudstone at Port-Eynon is preserved in a valley, suggesting that a landscape shaped like today's was then already in existence. Almost certainly, it was covered by more extensive later deposits that have since been eroded. Erosion in desert landscapes creates pediments – extensive, low-angled slopes – as higher ground is worn away. The 180m, 130m and 60m platforms of Gower may be remnants of Triassic desert pediments that have been uncovered from beneath younger rocks. They have also been interpreted as products of marine erosion, and indeed marine erosion during the Tertiary period (65 to 2 million years ago) may have removed the younger, less resistant rocks.

The final events in the geological history of Gower have taken place in

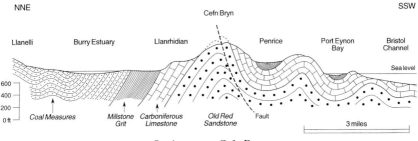

NNE   SSW
                                          Cefn Bryn

Llanelli   Burry Estuary   Llanrhidian   Penrice   Port Eynon   Bristol
                                                                         Bay   Channel

                                                                                    Sea level
  600
  400
  200
   0 ft   Coal Measures   Millstone Carboniferous   Old Red   Fault
                                 Grit   Limestone   Sandstone   3 miles

Section across Cefn Bryn

the last 2 million years, during the Pleistocene, the time of the Ice Ages. There have been several cold, glacial episodes, when ice sheets and glaciers covered most of Britain, including Gower, and sea-level was much lower than today because much of the water was locked up on land as ice. In between there have been shorter interglacials, with conditions of climate and sea-level like we are familiar with today. Many people are of the opinion that we live in an interglacial – the Holocene – which began only about 11,000 years ago, and there is no reason to think the ice ages are over.

Early in the Pleistocene, an ice sheet in the Irish Sea area spread south-east across Pembrokeshire and Gower bringing far-travelled erratic pebbles. Later ice sheets over mid-Wales and the Brecon Beacons pushed southwards on to the northern part of Gower bringing a mixture of rock debris from the South Wales Coalfield area. The deposits left by the glaciers are usually relatively thin and unconsolidated and so are referred to as superficial or drift deposits. Glaciers also extended down the Tawe and Neath valleys and out onto the floor of Swansea Bay, scouring hollows in the sea floor off Mumbles Head.

These ice masses provided meltwater for erosion of many valley features in both lowland and upland Gower. The steep western slopes of Rhossili Down were subjected to saturated flowage of rock debris (solifluction) over a frozen subsoil to form the pronounced terrace at the foot of the Down. A terrace at the foot of the cliffs at Oxwich Green had a similar origin and inland, the long gentle slopes of Cefn Bryn, Hardings Down and Rhossili Down were smoothed by solifluction.

Most of the limestone cliffs of Gower must be considered to be fossil as in most places they are not now attacked by the sea. A beach platform was cut in them before the Pleistocene, but today the sea only attacks a low cliff of solifluction debris lying at the foot of slopes leading up to the plateau. Accumulations of frost-shattered debris in the form of scree that may have originated during the cold climate of the Pleistocene are common below buttresses of limestone.

During the Pleistocene, with much water held on land as ice, sea level was lowered to expose the floor of the (now) Bristol Channel. Fine silty material (loess), blown from deposits on river beds draining from the ice sheet, lightly covers parts of the southern cliffs of Gower. Some 125,000 years ago sea level was higher than now, leaving beach materials, including sand, pebbles and limpet shells perched on a shore platform about 10m above present sea level. These 'raised beaches' were subsequently cemented with calcium carbonate which enabled them to survive to the present day. Caves cut by the sea at this period were subsequently occupied by now extinct animal species and their prey, such as rhinoceros, hyena, mammoth and bison. A skeleton found in 1823 by Dean Buckland at Paviland Cave became known as the 'red lady' of Paviland. The lady turned out to be male and recently was dated to 24,000 years before the present, confirming that human habitation of Gower has a very long history.

After climatic conditions improved and the glaciers melted, sea level rose in the Flandrian transgression until it reached approximately the present position. As the waters rose, masses of sand were driven landward and have come to rest at Pennard, Oxwich, Port-Eynon, Llangennith and Broughton Burrows. Overgrazed in the 16th century, and driven by a period of extra storminess, these dunes became mobile again and swamped Pennard castle. Towards the rear of Swansea Bay, dunes covered woodland, the stumps of which are being re-exposed by the sea and are referred to as the 'submerged forest'.

On the northern side of Gower, sediments accumulated to form Llanrhidian Marshes in the Burry Estuary. The sediment was derived mainly from erosion of the glacial deposits and later from soils as agricultural activities disturbed the natural environment. The marsh landscape of winding creeks and salt pans is a haven for wildfowl and is grazed by semi-wild ponies.

In summary, the scenery of Gower is characterised by a fairly level plateau surface some 60m above sea level, from which higher ground rises to about 120m on the commons of east Gower and to 180m on the summits of Cefn Bryn, Rhossili, Llanmadoc and Hardings Downs. The south and west coasts have steep cliffs and sandy bays but the north coast slopes down to the Burry estuary with its salt marshes. All these topographical features including their rocks, fossils and geological structure tell of a history stretching back over 400 million years.

E. M. Bridges and G. Owen

References

Bridges, E. M. 1970. The shape of Gower. *Gower* 21.
Bridges, E. M. 1985. Gower: the ice age limit. *Gower* 36.
Bridges, E. M. 1998. Classic Landforms of the Gower Coast, Geographical Association, Sheffield.
Culver, S. J. 1976. The development of the Swansea Bay area during the past 20,000 years. *Gower* 27.
Fielding, M. 1979. The glacial drainage channels of the City of Swansea. *Gower* 30.
Harris, C. 1974. Oxwich Burrows. *Gower* 25.
Owen, T. R. 1971. The structure of Gower. *Gower* 22.
Owen, T. R. 1972. The Carboniferous Limestone of Gower. *Gower* 23.
Owen, T. R. 1973. Geology and Scenery in the City of Swansea, *Gower* 24.

THE LORDSHIP OF GOWER

The marcher or seignorial lordship of Gower was founded by the Normans in the early twelfth century. It is not always recognised that historically and conceptually the lordship was far more extensive than the Gower peninsula. As well as the latter it included a large upland region, roughly bounded by the rivers Llwchwr, Aman, Twrch and Tawe. It also included the territory which lay east of the Tawe, between that river and Pwll Cynon, namely, the manor of Kilvey which, from the Norman period was associated with the lordship.

The lordship, which was 202 sq. miles in area, was broadly divided into two distinct and contrasting regions: the Anglo-Norman area of the lowland plateau and the interior upland zone. The former came to be designated as *Gower Anglicana* (or English Gower) and represented that part of the lordship which underwent the most intensive phase of Normanisation in terms of manorialism, nucleated settlements and the cultivation of crops. This was most pronounced in the Peninsula though *Anglicana* also included most of the land that came to form the ecclesiastical parish of Llandeilo Talybont.

By contrast *Gower Wallicana* (or Welsh Gower) on which this article concentrates, primarily embraced the upland region of the lordship and was almost equal in size to the peninsula. There was thus a co-incidence between lowland and Englishry and upland and Welshry. In Gower, the Welshry was sub-divided into *Subboscus* and *Supraboscus* (in Welsh, *Iscoed* and *Uwchcoed*), which in the specific conditions of Gower can be translated as the *'lower and upper parts of the Welshry wood'*.

According to Clarence Seyler, writing in 1925, 'the line separating *Subboscus* and *Supraboscus* was roughly the valley through which the railway . . . (runs) from Blackpill to Gowerton'. Today this is a cycle track which forms part of the Clyne Valley Country Park. *Subboscus* was that portion of *Iscoed* which was retained by Welsh tenants after the creation of the English county of Gower in the twelfth century. The nucleus of *Subboscus* was the ecclesiastical parish of Llanrhidian (Higher) and part of Loughor parish south of the Lliw and Llan rivers. *Supraboscus* essentially comprised the area covered by the ecclesiastical parishes of Llangyfelach and Llangiwg and was an area in which Norman influence was minimal and where the centralising forces that produced castle, church, manor and nucleated settlement were at their weakest. Unlike *Gower Anglicana*, *Supraboscus* was not socially organised in terms of compact manors but consisted of a large number of dispersed freeholdings which were subject to the payment of a small quit rent. Single farms were the dominant element in the upland zone, which was Welsh in language and culture, the only coherent territorial holdings being the former *maerdrefi* of the Welsh lords which were retained as desmesne lands by their Norman successors. One such estate was Trewyddfa.

Medieval sources reveal however that the original area of the lordship

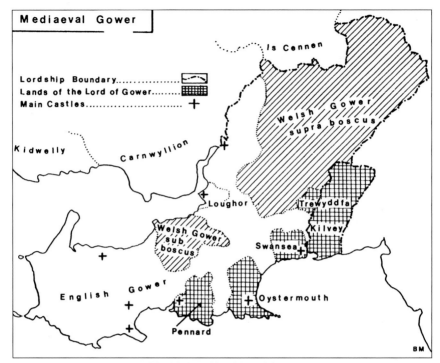

The Medieval Lordship of Gower

was more extensive than what it later came to cover. The boundary between the lordship and the Deheubarth commote of Is Cennen (itself part of Cantref Bychan) was initially marked by the river Aman. The boundary later moved southwards to the Nant Cathan, the present delimitation in these parts.

Between the Aman and Cathan lies Mynydd y Bettws and much of what became the ecclesiastical parish of Bettws, a territory which in the medieval period was also known as Stryveland. Overlooking the source of the Cathan is Penlle'r castell, the highest sited castle in Glamorgan, at 370m. above sea level. Lying on very exposed ground it has been described as 'an enigmatic structure' and was evidently constructed by one who conceded the need for a defensive structure built well within the original boundary of the lordship which would control the approaches to the latter from the north. The northern end of the ridge of Mynydd y Gwair provided a favourable location.

The castle, which was occupied for a relatively short duration, was constructed at a commanding position upon what remained until modern times an important trackway. It was erected in the second half of the thirteenth century, possibly as a temporary strongpoint during a localised border dispute – which became part of wider 'national' events involving the Crown and the Welsh princes – between William de Braose (1241-91), the Anglo-

Norman lord of Gower, and Rhys Fychan (*d.*1271), lord of Dinefwr. The latter was grandson of Rhys Grug (*d.*1234) and great-grandson of Rhys ap Tewdwr, the Lord Rhys (*d.*1197). Rhys Fychan was in large measure pursuing a policy of upholding the traditions of his illustrious forebears and faced with an unstable, disturbed frontier, de Braose may have conceded the necessity for a withdrawal from the Aman to the Cathan.

The majority of *Supraboscus* lay over 200m. above sea level, reaching heights of 300m. on broad wind-blasted summits such as Mynydd y Gwair, Mynydd Carnllechart, Mynydd y Garth, Penlle'rfedwen and Mynydd Allt-y-grug. Being situated in the western sector of the South Wales coalfield the area was totally underlain by rocks of the carboniferous system, in particular the Pennant and Upper Coal Series. It is the hard Pennant sandstone, comprising as it does the chief coal seams of the district, which gave rise to the monotonous tract of moorland that dominates much of the undulating topography of this part of the lordship.

The agricultural economy of *Supraboscus* was profoundly influenced by the physical environment, whilst the limitations set by climate, topography and soils were reflected in terms of settlement, landholding patterns and modes of husbandry. Although the soils could vary quite considerably in composition and texture they were predominantly clayey and sandy. By overlying the coal measures they were, in addition, often very thin, making them unsuitable for arable cultivation. Agriculturally *Supraboscus* was an area dominated by moorland and meadow, rough pasture and the sheepwalk. Being also a landscape of *small* hill farms and dispersed rural settlement, it was representative of upland districts generally. It is not surprising, therefore, that the emphasis was on pastoral farming and that the area was particularly susceptible to encroachment and other 'insidious ingressions'.

In earliest times most of this region was thickly forested with damp oak-wood, degenerating to alder scrub in the wetter parts. Traces of prehistoric settlements occur only at high levels on the vast open moorland. There is, for example, the Pontardawe Group of cairns comprising 27 sites, seven being ring circles, the most famous being Carn Llechart, one of the most impressive Bronze Age monuments in Glamorgan, consisting of a ring of 25 upright slabs enclosing a central burial cist. A short distance away is an even earlier sepulchral monument – a ruined Neolithic tomb – though it has been much disturbed. This part of *Supraboscus*, namely Mynydd Carnllechart, is replete with cairns and circles. A cairn cemetery exists near Brynchwith Farm and Baran Chapel whilst there is a cairnfield at Pwllfa Watkin close to the boundary with Llangiwg parish, which itself has many survivals on Penlle'rfedwen, Mynydd y Garth, Cefn Gwrhyd and Mynydd Allt-y-grug.

Other cairns survive on Banc Sion (near Penlle'r castell) and at Torclawdd on Mynydd y Gwair. There is also a Bronze Age burial mound on Mynydd Garngoch which also has remnants of miniature Roman fort practice camps whilst at Pantyfaa near Felindre and close to the boundary between Llangyfelach and Llandeilo Talybont parishes, there is a large cairn standing on a platform of stones. Further examples of cairns and/or rings are to be found on Graig Fawr (above Pontardulais), Cefn Drum (above Cwm Dulais), Penlle'r bebyll on Mynydd Pysgodlyn (above Felindre), Pen y Cwar (above Garnswllt) and Mynydd Garn Fach, above the Upper Lliw reservoir.

Jeff Childs

Grid References for Selected Locations within the Lordship of Gower:

Banc Sion	679086	Mynydd Allt-y-grug	752078	Pantyfaa	631029
Baran Chapel	687078	Mynydd Carnllechart	694073	Pen y Cwar	633080
Brynchwith Farm	686080	Mynydd Garn Fach	651064	Penlle'r bebyll	635048
Carn Llechart	697063	Mynydd Garngoch	606980	Penlle'r castell	665096
Cefn Drum	618046	Mynydd y Bettws	670106	Penlle'rfedwen	728111
Felindre	638027	Mynydd y Garth	713084	Pwllfawatkin	695083
Graig Fawr	623072	Mynydd y Gwair	665075	Torclawdd	670063
Llandeilo Talybont	585020	Mynydd y Gwrhyd	733095	Trewyddfa	663974
Llangiwg	724056				
Llangyfelach	646990				

References

Davis, Paul, 1997. *Historic Gower.*
Francis, G. G., 1861, *The Lordship of Gower in the Marches of Wales.*
Francis, G. G. & Baker, C., 1870, *Surveys of Gower & Kilvey.*
Powell, Gabriel, 1764, *Survey of Gower.*
Beverley Smith, J. & Pugh, T. B., 1971, *The Lordship of Gower & Kilvey in the Middle Ages.*
Glamorgan County History III: *The Middle Ages.*

GOWER PREHISTORY AND HISTORY

Weobley Castle

When the last of the great Ice Ages still maintained cold conditions over the whole of Western Europe, mammoth, bison and reindeer survived in large numbers. Even in the few slightly warmer intervals the human population of Britain consisted of only a few scattered families relying for life on the animals they could hunt, and the berries and plants they could gather. Flint tools made by these people have been found in several of the Gower caves, including Paviland and Longhole. When these caves were occupied, the Bristol Channel was a wide river valley, which supported animal and plant life to feed the cave dwellers, and the caves they used faced south, into the meagre warmth of the Ice Age sun. In Paviland Cave, sometime around 25,000 B.C., the skeleton of a young man had been buried with the skull of a mammoth at his feet and trinkets of bone about him. The bones, at first thought by the excavator to be those of a woman, were stained with red ochre, and thus the skeleton became known as the Red Lady of Paviland. These bones now rest in the University Museum at Oxford, and the Bristol Channel floods above his hunting ground.

The food-gathering life of these Stone Age people persisted with little change for many thousands of years, but a gradual improvement in climate and a slow increase in technical skill are indicated by discoveries of small, skilfully-worked flints on open sites such as Burry Holm, Llangennith, which may have been occupied about 10,000 B.C.

These smaller flints were intended to be mounted on wooden shafts, forming composite weapons and tools of considerable efficiency.

We are describing the peninsula of Gower, but we must here consider innovations which were being made far away in the Eastern Mediterranean, Mesopotamia and Egypt. In these areas some time after 10,000 B.C. men learned to sow and reap crops in due season, instead of relying on hunting or on casually gathering food from wild plants and trees. This led to an increase in living standards and in community life, and in the Middle East substantial cities were already flourishing by 3,000 B.C.

Gradually, agriculture as a basis for life extended across Europe, reaching Britain by about 4,000 B.C. Some early agriculturists spent considerable time and co-ordinated effort in constructing great communal tombs. These were built of massive slabs of stone covered with earth or stone mounds, and many were erected around the western coasts of Britain and have survived to our own time nearly 6,000 years later.

Most impressive of these tombs in Gower is Arthur's Stone on the high ridge of Cefn Bryn. A great 25-ton capstone still roofs the burial chamber. and the whole structure was once covered with a mound which has long since vanished. On the eastern slopes of Rhossili Down stand the Swine (or Sweyn's) Houses, two smaller tombs of similar type and date to Arthur's Stone, and on Penmaen Burrows, half buried in the dunes, there is a rather more complex tomb of the same period. This tomb has a stone-lined entrance passage, and a neat side chamber opening off the central area. The capstone of this tomb weighs 7 tons. Not far away, in the secluded Green Cwm behind Parkmill is the Giants' Grave, a sophisticated version of the Penmaen tomb, which still retains a large oblong stone mound around it. This tomb was restored following its excavation in 1960.

Giants' Grave, near Parkmill

Metal was unknown or at least not available to these early agriculturists, but soon after 2,000 B.C. users of copper, and in due course of bronze, appeared in Britain from North West Europe. These newcomers did not practise communal burial, but buried their dead singly beneath large earth or stone mounds, cremation becoming more frequent in later periods of the Bronze Age. Copper and bronze daggers and well-made pottery frequently accompanied the deceased in his last resting place. The edges of these burial mounds were often reused for burials later in this period. A fine mound of the Bronze Age can be seen near the main road at Cillibion (½ mile west of the road junction). Two other similar mounds were destroyed by the construction of Fairwood airfield.

The copper and bronze age lasted many centuries with a gradual increase in the skill and sophistication of the craftsmen, but the population of Britain in this period was probably not large. Few dwelling sites of this period have been discovered, but those which are known are usually unfortified.

By about 1,000 B.C. the population of Western Europe had increased, and competition for available land resulted in warfare between rival groups and tribes. This warfare and land shortage resulted in migration across the English Channel, and by 500 B.C. groups of these new warlike people were well established in Britain. They brought with them the knowledge of iron working, and as this metal was more readily obtainable than bronze, efficient implements of agriculture and of war became more generally available. These iron-using people defended themselves with fortifications, and many of these can still be seen. Cil Ifor hill fort is the finest in Gower, and consists of three great ramparts and ditches enclosing a steep-sided hill. Other impressive fortifications are to be found on Harding's Down. The Bulwark on Llanmadoc Hill is a more complex example. Although large, these forts were not fortified towns; perhaps their function should be compared with that of the communal air-raid shelters of World War II, not lived in normally but available to shelter the community in time of danger. As well as the large hill forts there are many smaller ring-works and promontory forts in the peninsula. These are usually the remains of small hamlets or farms defended by banks of ditches to give some small protection in troubled times.

The story of the many thousands of years we have described has been recovered by the skill of the archaeologist alone. No written records have survived from these times. During the Iron Age the expanding Roman civilisation reached Britain, and from this time written records give some assistance in tracing our story. References to Britain by Roman writers are few, and references to Wales are fewer. However, with the invasion of South Wales in 50 A.D. and the defeat of the dominant Iron Age tribe of the Silures we pass from prehistory to history.

When the Roman invasion forces arrived in South Wales the strongest tribe among the Iron Age peoples whose hill forts we have described was that of the Silures; and Gower was probably within their territory. Fierce resistance from the Silures delayed, but did not prevent, the Roman conquest of South Wales, and by 78 A.D. the Romans had established a pattern of military roads and forts which held Wales more or less under Roman rule for more than 300 years. The peninsula of Gower was by-passed by their military road, which ran through Neath, where the gateways of the fort still survive in a housing estate, to Loughor, and thence to Carmarthen. The Roman fort at Loughor lies below the medieval castle there and was extensively excavated in the 1980s. A Roman building stood at Oystermouth, where fragments of mosaic are on view in the Church, and above the quarry at Barland, Bishopston, Roman pottery, glass, charcoal and ironwork indicate that a settlement stood nearby in the 2nd century A.D.

When, in about 400 A.D., Rome finally abandoned Britain, South Wales reverted to the old Iron Age pattern of small independent kingdoms. Through these petty kingdoms, the great saints of the Celtic Church, Dewi, Teilo and Cadog, spread the Christian faith, and several of the Gower churches are dedicated to them. At Llanmadoc church a Christian tombstone survives from about 500 A.D., and at the Swansea Museum there is a Roman altar from Loughor which was re-used as a tombstone at the same date. Llangennith was the site of a small Celtic monastery founded by St. Cenydd in the 6th century, but destroyed by Viking raiders. The attacks of these pillaging seamen foreshadowed the advent of their ambitious and warlike relatives, the Normans. The Normans found the independent Welsh states little changed since they emerged in the 5th century. The small South Wales kingdoms were soon over-run by Norman lords, whose king allowed them to hold their conquests as Marcher Lordships, with powers approaching those of independent rulers. Soon after 1100, Gower had been annexed and had become a Norman Marcher Lordship, with the new town of Swansea as its fortress and capital. The Norman possession of Gower was neither undisputed nor secure, and successive attempts were made by the rulers of the Welsh states of Cardigan and the Vale of Towy to dislodge the invaders. At least six times between 1113 and 1217 the Welsh burned castles in Gower and devastated the countryside, but these attacks were raids and not reconquests. The castles which bore the brunt of this fighting were hastily constructed of turf and timber with earth and rubble defences, but towards the end of the 13th century the erection of the strong stone castles we see today marked the lasting triumph of the Normans. Although some were damaged during Owain Glyndŵr's revolt between 1400 and 1413, the construction of these stone castles marked the failure of Welsh resistance.

One result of the conquest was that Gower was thrown open to settlers from the West Country, and it is to the influx of English people at this time and to the subsequent cross-channel traffic that the distinctive character of the people and the peninsula is due. The medieval system of open field cultivation was practised extensively in the peninsula, and vestiges of it survive today, notably at Rhossili. The manorial system in the peninsula was Norman but in the parts of the Lordship north of Swansea, the old Welsh landholdings still survived into the 18th century. Within the peninsula, the limit of English colonisation appears to be defined by the belt of open moor formed by Clyne, Fairwood and Pengwern Commons, and by Welsh Moor. North of this line, although the land tenures were Norman, the population was, and is, largely Welsh in origin and outlook. This is the poorer land where the coal measures outcrop, and here, from the 16th century onwards coal has been worked and exported. At Penclawdd the only industrial centre in the peninsula was established, and from the 18th century the brass, copper, lead and coal industries brought prosperity to the area.

Away from the Penclawdd area, industry in Gower was limited to the extensive quarrying of limestone, much of which was shipped to limeless North Devon, and to the quarrying of red ochre or 'paint mineral'. The limestone industry was very active during the 19th century, and many of the derelict coastal quarries are easily recognised today. Oyster fishing was another important 19th century occupation and the remains of the perches, or storage pools, can still be seen at Port-Eynon and Mumbles. In recent years the coal-mines have been abandoned, the oysters are gone, and the limestone industry was first reduced to one large mechanised quarry which replaced the many small 'quars', and eventually ceased production. However, agriculture remains of major importance, as it has been since the first immigrant farmers erected Arthur's Stone so many years ago.

Bernard Morris

SEASHORE LIFE AND TIDES

There are a few different types of shore around the Gower peninsula, each with a different seashore community. On the north coast is the flat muddy estuarine shore of the Llwchwr (Loughor) river, and some of its tributaries such as the Burry. On the north-west coast and parts of the south coast are the sandy beaches so popular with tourists and day-trippers alike. At the top of many sandy shores are sand dunes, with a vast array of flowers and other plants. On the west and other parts of the south coast are rocky shores and limestone cliffs, most of which are 60 metres (200 feet) above sea level. Many sea birds and cliff dwelling birds nest on these. The rocky shores are the best for studying seashore life, since there is no sand or mud in which the animals can hide.

The rise and fall of the tides around the Gower coast varies considerably. Indeed, the Bristol Channel has the second highest tidal amplitude in the world. The spring tides are the ones with the greatest amplitude or range – the highest high tides and the lowest low tides. During the spring tides, the tidal range is sometimes over ten metres (33 feet). During the neap tides the range is a lot less. We are lucky in that the spring tides around the Gower coast have the low water at 12.00 to 2.00 o'clock (night and day) – and this is the time to be at the bottom of the shore looking for all the wildlife. Neap tides have their low water at about 6.00 to 8.00 o'clock. (N.B. If you wish to visit the tidal islands then Worms Head and Burry Holms are accessible for about 2½ hours each side of low water; Mumbles Head is accessible for about 1½ hours each side of low water.)

(*The number in brackets in the following paragraphs is a reference to a drawing at the end of this article.*)

Seaweeds grow on the rocky shores. They are algae, and do not have roots, so they cannot grow in sand or mud. There are three groups of seaweeds – green, brown and red. Most grow in well-defined zones on the shore. Of the green algae, the one at the top of the shore, and around freshwater runoffs, is gutweed (1). Sea lettuce (2) lives in the middle to lower shore, and is often abundant in rock pools. The dense tufts of fine green, wiry branched threads in some pools is *Cladophora* (3). The most obvious zonation is shown by the brown algae. The narrow-fronded, leathery channelled wrack is found highest on the shore, above the line of high water neap tides. At and below high water neap is the spiral wrack, the one with the swollen tips that look like heat-sealed polythene bags. Next down the shore comes the bladder wrack (4), with its air-filled floats in pairs. At mid tide level and below we get either saw wrack, or, on very sheltered shores, the knotted wrack (5), which has single air bladders. At low water spring tides we have the kelps or oarweeds. One of them, the sugar kelp (8), looks like a strip of puckered ribbon tapering to a root-like holdfast. Two other common ones, tangle and cuvie, have flat, broad blades, torn into strips by the action of the waves. Many beautiful red seaweeds grow in the rock pools, or on the rocks lower down the shore. There is the succulent pepper dulse (7), leaf-like dulse (9), feathery *Ceramium* (6), jointed coral weed (10), and crinkly forked Irish moss (11). The laverbread for sale in Swansea Market is made from a red alga, laver weed. This grows at and above mid tide level, a very thin, almost black or dark purple membrane lying on the rocks and stones. Seaweeds collected for mounting on paper should be kept in water and carefully floated on to the surface of the immersed paper. When dry they should be covered with transparent film or paper.

Animals on the seashore are varied and diverse. The shore is a very difficult environment in which to live, so the animals are all extremely well adapted to this, and no other, area.

Beginning with rocky shores, the rocks themselves are encrusted with acorn barnacles (12), especially higher on the shore. These are crustaceans, related to crabs and shrimps, but live a sedentary adult life in small conical shells cemented to the rock surface. Scurrying across the dry rocks at the top of the shore are sea slaters (18), the largest British woodlouse. Also on the rocks and in crevices may be found various molluscs which are relatives of the snail: limpets (14), periwinkles of all sizes and top shells (15) are all herbivores, feeding on the algae on the rocks when the tide is in. Dog whelks (16) are carnivores which feed on other molluscs and acorn barnacles; their cream or purple egg cases (17) are frequently found in clusters on the underside of rocks. Attached to the rocks by threads of protein are purple-blue mussels. These are bivalve molluscs, related to the cockle. Adhering to the rocks are another type of mollusc, the chitons (23), which are often mistaken for fossil woodlice. Below mid-tide level, there are a number of species of sponge growing. The most abundant on the exposed rock surfaces is the breadcrumb sponge, a creamy orange or pale green colour. Around the edges of rock pools is a different, bright orange species, *Hymeniacidon*. In the middle shore, where sand is carried amongst the boulders and rocks, you may find a mass of honeycomb-like tubes of the reef worm. They make their tubes by sticking sand grains together. Wriggling along the rock surface, often amongst the barnacles is the greenleaf worm, a bright green in colour. Under stones, especially in fine grain sand, we sometimes find the ragworm, a whitish pink colour, with its red dorsal blood vessel showing through its skin. Also under stones may be found various brittle stars (20), related to the starfish (which is not a seashore species – those found on the shore are usually weakened and dying). In rock pools you will find crustaceans such as prawns and hermit crabs (19) which use the shells of molluscs as a home. Under stones are other crustaceans such as the green shore crab, the pink edible crab and the very fierce blue and red fiddler or velvet crab, which has very flattened back legs. Young specimens are able to use these legs to swim. Low on the shore you will find the small broad-clawed porcelain crab, which is covered in hairs, and the even smaller long-clawed porcelain crab (13), which often pushes itself along backwards with its long claws. All crustaceans periodically moult their outside skeleton in order to grow, and seek shelter during this process. They are soft and very vulnerable until their new, larger, skeleton has hardened. Attached to the rocks are several types of sea anemones. The blobs of red or greenish jelly on the exposed rocks are the beadlet anemone – they open to reveal a circle of tentacles when under water. In pools you may well see iridescent green or dull red snakeslocks anemones (21). These have tentacles so long that they cannot withdraw them. Distantly related to the anemones is the stalked jellyfish (22), which is usually attached to seaweeds, and very difficult to see. The rockpool fish include the blenny (24), the bull-head, with a large head and spines on its gills, the rocklings (25), with barbels around their mouths, and the pipe fish (26), which is common, but often overlooked since it resembles a strand of sea weed.

The magnificent sandy beaches such as Swansea, Oxwich, Port-Eynon, Rhossili and the mud flats of the Burry Estuary, harbour a flourishing population of burrowing animals. Bivalve molluscs are numerous, and include razor shells (28), cockles and venus shells. Other bivalve shells will be found washed up on the strand line, including small tellin and wedge shells (29), and larger gapers (33), scallops and oysters. The fragile white piddock (31) will be found on some strand lines. Snail-type shells to seek include the cowries (30), large polished necklace shells, pink and white striped acteons, pointed tower shells (27), the ribbed spiral white wendletraps (32), and the slipper limpet (37), which was introduced from America, and resembles a Chinese slipper. A number of worms live in the sand, including the large greenish black lugworm, often sought for as bait, which throws up a coil of worm-like cast on the surface of the sand. The sand mason worm makes a tube by sticking sand grains and bits of shell together. The top of the tube is a fluffy fringe, and sticks up proud of the sand surface. The peacock worm (35) builds its tube from mud, and is only exposed by very low tides. When they are submerged, the worm pushes out a beautiful array of tentacles to trap food particles from the water.

Washed up after storms you may find several kinds of jellyfish, and the by-the-wind-sailor (38), with its beautiful violet oval membrane under a curved fin-like sail. The test of the sea potato (36), which is a species of sea urchin, is often found; it is very delicate and breaks easily. The horny black egg cases of the skate (39) and the softer translucent ones of the dogfish (40) are sometimes found. These are both called mermaid's purse. Oval pieces of white substance, hard on one side with soft lamellae on the other are the shells of the cuttlefish (34). These are collected to give to pet canaries and budgerigars which eat them to supplement the calcium in their diet. Loose balls of a membranous bubble-like material are the egg cases of the whelk (41).

Good hunting! However, a few words of advice: don't try to take fish or other animals home in jars, unless you have a seawater aquarium ready to receive them; they are not easy to keep. Also, after you have turned a stone over, please return it the right way up. There are many animals (some too small to see) which are living under the stone which will die if they are left exposed to the atmosphere. Tide tables can be purchased in a number of fishing and sports shops. They are also published in the local paper (the *South Wales Evening Post*). These give the times of high tides. Add six hours and ten minutes to estimate the time of low water. Aim to be on the shore before low water, and work your way down, to be at the tide's edge at the time of low water. That way you will see the animals and plants of the various levels of the shore – and I repeat, please return the stones after you have upturned them!

Michael Isaac

Some books which will help to identify
sea shore plants and animals:

'Collins Pocket Guide to the Sea Shore'. P. Hayward, T. Nelson-Smith & C. Shields. 1996. HarperCollins.

More detailed:
'A Student's Guide to the Sea Shore'. 1996. J. D. Fish & S. Fish. Cambridge University Press (this also gives some of the very interesting biology of the organisms).

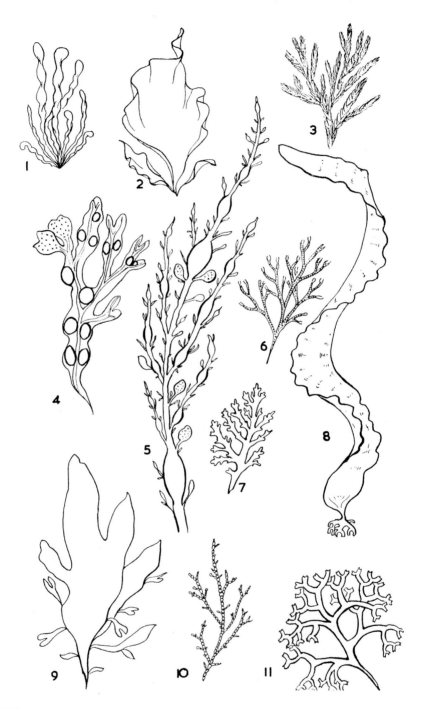

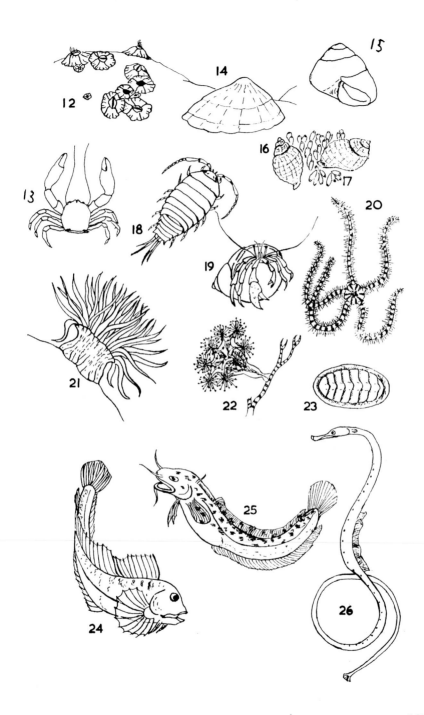

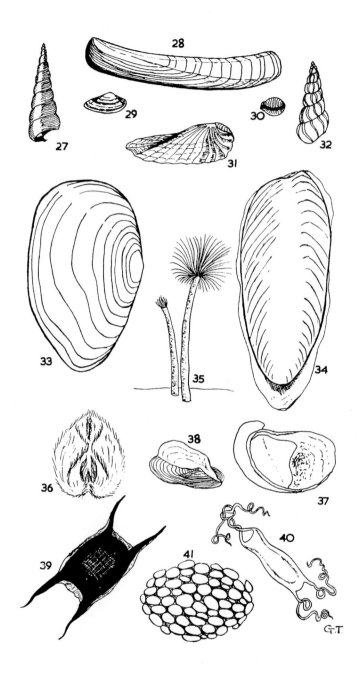

WALKING
IN GOWER

Gower is a small peninsula thrusting into the Bristol Channel just 14 miles long from Mumbles to Rhossili and six miles wide from Mumbles to Gowerton. The area is unique in the total and length of numbered footpaths and the range of landscapes through which the paths pass. There are nearly 400 miles of rights of ways in the Gower area; these transverse sandy beaches, small coves, magnificent cliffs, a patchwork pattern of fields and large stretches of open common. Because of the unspoiled nature of these areas, the Gower Peninsula was designated Britain's first Area of Outstanding Natural Beauty in 1956. There are more areas of Special Scientific Interest, Wildlife Trust Reserves and National Trust land in Gower than in any comparable size area in the country.

The size of the peninsula is such that a walk need not be exclusively inland or along the coast, even short walks can combine a variety of scenery. In addition, walking can be combined with other interests, such as history, geology, or bird life; in fact the articles in this Guide highlight the range of interests that can be followed during a walk in Gower.

Like anywhere in Britain, the weather can change suddenly, for better or for worse, it can even rain all day on occasions! Generally, however, the climate is mild with invigorating sea winds. Following a wet spell, footpaths can become very muddy; so it is advisable to be prepared with suitable wet weather gear and adequate footwear.

When walking through Gower's kaleidoscope of scenery, although it is very easy to be distracted and to forget the fundamentals of the Country Code (a copy in this Guide), you should make every effort to remember that Gower is still a working farming community. Remember also, one's right on a footpath is restricted to passage only along that path, it does not allow walkers or their dogs on to neighbouring property. Dogs must be kept under control at all times. Prior permission should always be obtained before you park in private car parks (e.g. pubs, shops, etc.) to go on a walk. If parking is allowed on the side of a road, lane or track take care not to cause an obstruction to villagers, farmers and other road users.

Unfortunately, space in this article is restricted, so only limited details for a small number of walks can be given.

The 1:25000 Ordnance Survey (O.S.) map of Gower, Explorer No. 10 (164), is highly recommended for anyone wanting to explore the network of footpaths. The smaller scale 1:50000 Landranger 159, 'Swansea, Gower and Surrounding Area', is useful for general planning of walks. Public rights of way are marked on all OS maps but many of these, if not waymarked, are difficult to follow on the ground

Many of the suggestions for walks in the original 'Guide to Gower' made use of the many bus routes which served Gower in the past. Unfortunately, bus services are more limited nowadays, and a great deal of ingenuity is required if without a car.

Circular walks of various lengths can be planned using the OS map Explorer 10, which shows rights of way, and some of the 23 suggested locations for starting and finishing given in the Reference Section of this Guide. The walks, using the extensive network of rights of way, can start and finish either at official Car Parks (where a fee may be charged) or at recognised parking places (where care should be taken not to obstruct lanes or field gates).

A combination of bus and car is sometimes possible by taking a bus to the far point of a walk and then walking back to the car. To obtain the up-to-date route numbers and times of buses contact the bus company 'First Cymru' on Swansea 01792 580580. For the starting points check the Gazetteer entry and/or maps.

There are many excellent books of walks now available (see Book List), two of which can be particularly recommended, namely 'Gower Walks' by Ruth Ridge published by The Gower Society and 'Walking Around Gower' published by the Ramblers' Association.

A list of selected car parks suitable for beginning walks is given in the Reference Section.

The following walk suggestions are based, in part, on original work by Bernard Morris and O.S. Map Explorer 10 (164) will help you to follow them:

Barland Common (Grid Reference 578869) **on B4436** go down towards Bishopston Church and then cross ford and follow old road up to Kittle. Turn down into Bishopston Valley and follow the valley to Pwlldu Bay, returning via Brandy Cove to Pyle Corner and along Bishopston Road to Barland Common (4 miles).

Penmaen, on A4118 (Parking places at Grid Reference 531888 & 528888). Go down lane towards Tor Bay. Just before a farm ruin, a footpath goes off on RHS. Proceed by field gates and stiles onto track through woodland high above Nicholston Burrows. Follow the track through the woods to Nicholaston. Cross the A4118 and follow footpaths at the base of Cefn Bryn to Penmaen (3m) or on ridge of Cefn Bryn, passing the Gower Way Stone to Penmaen (4m).

Parking Place at Millwood, near Penrice (Grid Reference 493883) Forestry Commission tracks passing Capon's Hill and up to Brynsil or to Penrice Church provide a number of circular walks through the woods of between 3m and 5m, returning via the old mill race and fish ponds.

Parking Place at Arthur's Stone (Grid Reference 492900) by footpaths to Reynoldston Police Station, on A4118. Cross road with care and go S. down a rough track into Mill Wood. Follow Forestry Commission tracks and footpaths to Kittle Top before returning by footpaths to the parking place (4m).

Penmaen Church on A4118 (Parking Places at Grid Reference 531888 & 528888) along green track on the ridge of Cefn Bryn. Follow the ridgeway (Talbot's Road) to Arthur's Stone (alternative parking place at Grid Reference 492900) and Frog Moor. Then follow footpaths to Reynoldston and return to Talbot's Road and so back to parking at Arthur's Stone (4m) or to Penmaen (8m).

Llanmadoc P.O. or **Cheriton** (Private Parking Area with Honesty Box at G.R. 439935) by footpath to Llanmadoc Hill, across Tankeylake Moor to Hardings Down and Cathan. Follow track to Whitemoor. Climb across open moorland to top of Rhossili Down and walk along ridge to Llangennith and back onto Llanmadoc Hill to return to Llanmadoc (7m).

Pilton Green on B4247, Rhossili road (parking at Grid Reference 446871) S. along waymarked footpath to cliff path, near the descent to Paviland Cave. Thence E. along coast to Overton to return on footpaths via Hills and Paviland Manor Farms (6m).

The South Coast Cliff Path. A footpath follows the south coast all the way from Mumbles to Rhossili – about 25m of rough but rewarding walking. It is sometimes walked from end to end in one day – but consists of many easily followed convenient sections which provide excellent shorter walks.

The following walks are not circular and will require a bus or combination of bus and car:

From **Overton**, W. along lane/footpath leading W. over the magnificent cliffs to Rhossili (6m).

From **Cartersford on B4271**, go N.W. past East Hills and Little Hills to Bryn, then across to Welsh Moor along a minor metalled road to Llanrhidian (5m).

From **Junction of Kittle Hill Lane with A4118**, go W. past Courthouse to Ilston thence down Ilston Valley to Parkmill (5m).

From **Cillibion on B4271**. By footpath S.W. along the edge of Decoy Wood and through Lodge Cwm into Park Woods (Green Cwm) and thence to Parkmill (2¾m). Alternatively, this walk can be started at Llethrid Bridge going via Llethrid Cwm into Park Woods (2m).

From **Stembridge on road to Llangennith**, N.W. over Ryer's Down to Cheriton (2m), Llanmadoc (2½m), or along the top of Llanmadoc Hill to Llangennith (3½m).

From **Llangennith Bus Terminus**. N.W. via Cockstreet and a footpath to Broughton Bay, thence by footpath high up on Broughton Burrows follow the coast to Burry Holm. Then walk S. along Rhossili Sands to Diles Lake, and follow track N.E. to metalled lane heading back to Llangennith (5m).

From **Knelston on A4118**, by footpath S. to Berry thence by green lanes to Horton (3m).

From **Llandewi Corner on A4118**, W. along green lane to Old Henllys and Kingshall and thence by footpath to the top of Rhossili Down and Rhossili (4m). (*This is on the route of The Gower Way*).

The Editors

BOOK LIST

Books about Gower have been published in increasing numbers during recent years. The Gower Society itself publishes many. Inevitably the older books are now out of print, but almost all may be consulted at the Central Library reference room in Alexandra Road, Swansea. Many of the sources mentioned below have been used in the preparation of this guide. The Society's Journal *Gower* is published annually in November and contains much new research and general information about Gower. Many of the earlier volumes are now available only at libraries, but the Gower Society still has some for sale.

In 1998 the Swansea Libraries Local Studies Service, in conjunction with the Gower Society's Golden Jubilee, produced a selected list of books on Gower which are available for consultation at Swansea Reference Library. The list includes many of the books listed below and more.

Some of the articles in *A Guide to Gower* include a bibliography of sources relating to that article.

Historical
A History of Swansea and the Lordship of Gower: W. H. Jones, 1920 (Vol. I); 1992 (Vol. II).
Penard and West Gower: Latimer Davies, 1928.
★*Gower Gleanings*: Horatio Tucker, 1951.
My Gower: Horatio Tucker, 1957.
The Mumbles, Past and Present: N. L. Thomas, 1978.
A History of Bishopston: Geoffrey R. Orrin, 1982.
A Gower Family (The Lucases of Stouthall & Rhossili Rectory): Robert Lucas, 1986.
The Story of the Village of Mumbles: Gerald Gabb, 1986, ISBN 0 905928 61 X.
A Pictorial Journey Through Edwardian Gower: David Gwynn & Peter Muxworthy, 1989, ISBN 0 86383 422 1.
The Penrice Letters 1768-1797: edited by Joanna Martin, 1993.
Edwardian Gower Revisited: David Gwynn & Peter Muxworthy, 1994. ISBN 1 85902 153 0.
A Childhood in Mumbles & Gower: Freda Marrison, 1995.
Historic Gower: Paul Davies, 1997, ISBN 0 7154 0732 5.
★*Old Gower Farmhouses*: Bernard Morris, 1998, ISBN 0 902767 18 6.
Higher and Lower (A History of Llanrhidian): R. N. Cooper, 1998. ISBN 0 9534 523 0 1.
Pwlldu Remembered: Heather Holt, 1996. ISBN 0 9529165 0 9.

Topographical and General
★*Swansea Bay to Worms Head*: Photographs and drawings, 1963.
★*The Castles of Gower*: Bernard Morris & Harold Grenfell, 1970.
★*The Caves of Gower*: Bernard Morris & Harold Grenfell, 1971.
Swansea & Its Region: W. G. V. Balchin (ed.), University College of Swansea, 1971.
A Gower Anthology: David Rees (ed.), 1977.
The Men of the Mumbles Head: Carl Smith, 1977.
Gower Shipwrecks: P. H. Rees, 1978.
The Gower Churches: Geoffrey R. Orrin, 1979.

The Gower Coast: George Edmunds, 1979.
*_Noteworthy Gower Churches_: L. A. Toft & Harold Grenfell, 1981.
*_The Sea Beneath My Feet_: J. Mansel Thomas, 1981.
Portrait of Gower: Wynford Vaughan Thomas, (2nd. edition), 1983. ISBN 0 709155 77 8.
Rhossili: Robert Lucas, 1989. ISBN 0 905928 93 8.
A Journey Through Gower: H. Middleton-Jones, 1991(reprint). ISBN 0 7154 0716 3.
*_Gower Walks_: Ruth Ridge, 1st. edition: 1991. ISBN 0 902767 12 7.
                                    2nd. edition: 1999. ISBN 0 902767 22 4.
Gower Coast Shipwrecks: Carl Smith, 1993. ISBN 0 9515281 4 983.
Gowerland & Its Language: Robert Penhallurick (1994).
A Swansea Anthology: James A. Davies (ed.), 1997. ISBN 1 85411 175 2.
Three Corners of Gower: Peter R. Douglas-Jones, 1997. ISBN 0 9532038 0 8.
Walking Around Gower. The Ramblers' Association, (3rd. edition), 1998. ISBN 0 9518780 1 8.
Reynoldston: Robert Lucas, 1998.

Geology and Natural History
Geologists' Association Guide No. 17: The Swansea District by T. R. Owen & F. H. T. Rhodes.
The Glamorgan County History, Vol. I, 1936.
*_Plant Life in Gower_: G. T. Goodman, 1961.
Geology Explained in South Wales by T. R. Owen, 1973.
The Natural History of Gower: Mary F. Gillham, 1983 (reprint). ISBN 0 905928 00 8.
Wildlife in Glamorgan: Nigel A. Lewis (ed.), 1991. ISBN 0 9508245 7 7.
Classic Landforms of the Gower Coast: E. M. Bridges, 1997. ISBN 1 899085 50 5.

* Gower Society publications.

SELECTED CAR PARKS
for STARTING WALKS

National Trust Car Park at Pennard. (*Charge*). (Grid Reference 554874).
Municipal Car Park at Horton. (*Charge*). (Grid Reference 473855).
Municipal Car Park at Port-Eynon. (*Charge*). (Grid Reference 468851).
Municipal Car Park at Caswell. (*Charge*). (Grid Reference 595857).
Private Parking Area at Llanmadoc. (*Honesty Box*). (Grid Reference 439935).
Private Parking Area at Great Pitton. (*Honesty Box*). (Grid Reference 427876).
Private Parking Area at Oxwich. (*Charge*). (Grid Reference 502845).
(*N.B. opening times limited*).
Private Parking Area at Rhossili. (*Charge*). (Grid Reference 416880).
Private Parking Area at Rhossili Church. (*Honesty Box*). (Grid Reference 417881).
Public Car Park at Penclawdd. (Grid Reference 545959).
Public Car Park at Dunvant. (Grid Reference 595939).
Parking Place near Arthur's Stone. (Grid Reference 492900).
Parking Place at Barland Common. (Grid Reference 578869).
Parking Place at Blue Anchor. (Grid Reference 554948).
Parking Place at Burry Green. (Grid Reference 462914).
Parking Place at Fairwood Common. (Grid Reference 568923).
Parking Place at Landimore. (Grid Reference 466933).
Parking Place at Millwood, near Penrice. (Grid Reference 493883).
Parking Place at Mount Hermon Chapel, Penclawdd. (Grid Reference 533954).
Parking Place (*very limited*) **at Ryers Down.** (Grid Reference 449922).
Parking Places (2) at Penmaen. (Grid Reference 531888 & 528888).
Parking Place at Pilton Green. (Grid Reference 446871).
Forestry Parking Area at Parkmill. (Grid Reference 538896).

Note: *Motorists should always ensure that car doors are locked and that belongings are secured out of sight. This is particularly important when parked at remote or unattended sites.*

GETTING ABOUT
BY PUBLIC TRANSPORT IN GOWER

The public transport services operating in and to Gower have undergone many alterations in the last few years and are likely to continue to undergo changes in the future; therefore, times or service numbers for buses have not been included in this edition of *A Guide to Gower*. For the most up to date information it is best to enquire from **First Cymru Bus Service** on **01792 580 580** or from the **Swansea Tourist Information Centre** on **01792 468 321**.

LEISURE ACTIVITIES

It is possible to enjoy a wide range of leisure activities in Gower, both organised activities and those which appeal to the solitary visitor. However, it should be remembered that, as well as an excellent holiday location, Gower is both the home and the working environment of many people and the Country Code (see Reference Section) should be followed at all times. The following list gives an indication of what is available. Contact telephone numbers are given and more information can be obtained from the City & County of Swansea web site at http://www.swansea.gov.uk or from the Swansea Tourist Information Centre (tel: 01792 468 321 fax: 01792 464602).

- Angling: City & County of Swansea Fishing Permits Office; tel: 01792 635 436.

- Birdwatching: The Wildfowl & Wetlands Trust, Llanelli; tel: 01554 741 087.

- Caving/Rock Climbing: Swansea Tourist Information Centre; tel: 01792 468 321.

- Canoeing: Wales Leisure Activities; tel: 01792 296 769.

- Cycling: A cycling guide is available from Swansea Tourist Information Centre; tel: 01792 468 321.

- Diving: Swansea Yacht & Sub Aqua Club; tel: 01792 654863 or Swansea Tourist Information Centre

- Flying: Swansea Aero Club & Flying School; tel: 01792 204063.

- Golf: Swansea Tourist Information Centre; tel: 01792 468 321.

- Horse Riding/Pony Trekking: Swansea Tourist Information Centre; tel: 01792 468 321.

- Sailing/Water Skiing: for details contact Swansea Tourist Information Centre; tel: 01792 468 321.

- Surfing/Wind Surfing: The Welsh Surfing Federation; tel: 01656 784 874 or Swansea Tourist Information Centre; tel: 01792 468 321.

- Walking: A leaflet listing guided walks is available from the City & County of Swansea Countryside Service; tel: 01792 635 714. See also the Book List, the Walks article in this guide and the walks programmes of the Gower Society & the Ramblers' Association West Glamorgan Group.

- Youth Hostelling: YHA, Port-Eynon 01792 390706.

Tourist Literature & Publications:

The Swansea Tourist Information Centre has a number of free information leaflets together with others for which a charge is made. Tide Tables may be purchased at many local shops.

NATIONAL TRUST PROPERTIES IN GOWER

(See map page 120)

Name	Grid References	Description
Llanrhidian Marsh	435 985- 580 967	Grazed salt marsh. A site of international importance for wading birds & for wildfowl
Whiteford Burrows & Cwm Ivy Marsh, & Tor	445 940–435 943	The burrows form an extensive dune system and the marsh is pasture backed by woodland and limestone cliffs
Rhossili	410 886	Dramatic cliff headlands & foreshore with views to Lundy Island
South Gower Coast	420 871	Dramatic cliffs & views to North Devon
Nicholaston, Penmaen & Three Cliff Bay	526 879–538 880	Vegetated dunes & sandy coves leading round headland to Three Cliff Bay
Pennard Cliffs	555 870	High rugged cliffland of considerable geological interest
Bishopston Valley & Pwlldu	575 870	Secluded wooded valley with stream running down to shingle banked beach. Remarkable limestone geological structure throughout the valley

For additional information, including notes on facilities, access, natural history, geology and archaeology, see the National Trust leaflet **'Properties to Visit on Gower'** *or contact the National Trust Warden at Little Reynoldston Farm, Reynoldston, Gower SA3 1AQ (tel: 01792 390636).*

THE NATURE RESERVES IN GOWER OF THE GLAMORGAN WILDLIFE TRUST

(See map page 120)

Note: *The following list is for information of location only. It must not be taken as implied permission to visit any of the reserves. The reserves are the property of the Glamorgan Wildlife Trust, telephone 01656 724100.*

The editors acknowledge, with thanks, permission from the Glamorgan Wildlife Trust to use extracts from their book 'Where to Go for Wildlife in Glamorgan', edited by Nigel A. Lewis. The book contains much information on the reserves in Gower as well as on many more in the former county of Glamorgan.

Name of Reserve	Grid Reference	Acreage	Optimum Times of Year to Visit
Berry Wood, Knelston	474 884	16.9	April–July *Woodland flowers & birds*; Sept.–Oct. *Fungi*
Betty Church Reserve, Cwm Ivy	440 937	5.5	April–July *Flowers & birds*; May–Sept. *Meadows*; Sept.–Oct. *Fungi*
Broad Pool & Bog	510 910	4.2	May–Aug. *Aquatic flowers & dragon flies*; Sept.–April *Migrants & wintering raptors*
Bunker's Hill, Pitton	428 881	0.7	April–June *Spring flowers*; Sept.–Nov. *Fungi*
Castle Wood Field, Landimore	472 931	0.8	April–July *Salt Marsh Flowers*; May–July *Summer coastal birds*
Cwm Ivy Woods	443 939	27.4	March– June *Woodland flowers*; May–July *Woodland birds*; Sept.–Nov. *Fungi*
Elizabeth & Rowe Harding Reserve, Ilston	555 905	4.9	April–June *Spring flowers*; June–July *Birds*
Gellihir Woods, Fairwood Common	562 925	70.8	April–July *Flowers, butterflies, birds*; Sept.–Nov. *Fungi*
Hambury Woods, Landimore	472 929	11.8	April–July *Flowers & birds*; Sept.–Nov. *Fungi*
Kilvrough Manor Woods	555 892	18.5	April–June *Flowers*; June–July *Birds*

Name of Reserve	Grid Reference	Acreage	Optimum Times of Year to Visit
Llanrhidian Hill	495 922	7.6	April–June *Spring flowers*; June–July *Summer birds*; Sept.–Nov. *Fungi*
Lucas Reserve, Frog Lane, Llanmadoc	447 933	1.1	March–June *Flowers*; June–July *Birds*
Peel Wood, Oystermouth	607 883	2.8	April–June *Flowers*; June–July *Birds*; Sept.–Nov. *Fungi*
Prior's Wood & Meadow, Three Crosses	577 938	4.3	March–June *Flowers*; June–July *Birds*; Sept.–Nov. *Fungi*
Redden Hill Wood, Parkmill	538 894	2.8	April–June *Flowers*; May–June *Birds & butterflies*; Sept.–Nov. *Fungi*
Redley Cliff, Caswell Bay	589 875	9.0	April–July *Coastal flowers*; May–July *Coastal birds*
Ridgewood Park, Mayals	611 906	0.8	April–June *Flowers*; June–July *Suburban birds*; Sept.–Nov. *Fungi*
South Gower Coast – Deborah's Hole	435 862	16.5	April–July *Flowers*; June–July *Coastal birds*
South Gower Coast – Long Hole Cliff	450 850	50.2	March–June *Coastal flowers*; May–July *Birds*; Nov.–March *Sea watching*
South Gower Coast – Overton Cliff	458 848	23.2	April–June *Flowers*; May–July *Coastal birds*
South Gower Coast – Overton Mere	462 848	28.6	March–July *Coastal flowers*; May–July *Birds*
South Gower Coast – Port Eighteen Point	465 845	33.0	Jan.–Feb. *Wintering divers, etc.*; March–June *Coastal flowers*; May–July *Birds*; July–August *Sea watching for bird movement (best at daybreak)*
South Gower Coast – Sedges Bank	470 844	86.7	At low tide–*Sub littoral animals & plants*; May–July *Birds*; Sept.–March *Migratory birds & grey seals*